classic BEETLE

a VW celebration

First published in the
United Kingdom in 2015 by
Pavilion
1 Gower Street
London
WC1E 6HD

Copyright ©
Pavilion Books Company Ltd 2015
Text copyright ©
Pavilion Books Company Ltd 2015

Produced for Pavilion by Essential Works
www.essentialworks.co.uk
Images on pages 19, 25, 27, 30, 33, 38, 43,
44 and 46 courtesy of magiccarpics.com,
images on pages 50 and 53 courtesy of
Associated News.

ISBN 978-1-910496-61-9

A CIP catalogue record for this book is
available from the British Library.

10 9 8 7 6 5 4 3 2 1

Reproduction by
Mission Productions Ltd, Hong Kong
Printed and bound by
1010 Printing International Ltd, China

This book can be ordered direct from the
publisher at www.pavilionbooks.com

classic BEETLE

a VW celebration

keith sueme

foreword brian laban

contents

the cars

the details

foreword

For almost half of the 20th century, the Volkswagen Beetle was "The People's Car". Against extraordinary odds, an intensely austere design conceived in pre-World War II Germany not only survived that global conflict in which Germany was comprehensively defeated, but was re-born after it, largely through the efforts of Germany's wartime enemies; it found markets around the world, and survived for almost another 60 years, into a new century.

In all that time, what became known as the Beetle kept pace with the rest of the motoring world so far as it had to, while always remaining instantly recognizable as an evolution of the original concept, laid down by Ferdinand Porsche in the mid-1930s. As conceived, it satisfied political ambition by replacing small-car convention with brilliant mechanical innovation, but it was the Volkswagen's practicality and dependability rather than any lack of it that underpinned its long-term global success.

Its genesis was underwritten by Adolf Hitler's vision of a *Volksauto*, its wartime survival was guaranteed by the excellence of its military variants, its rebirth was engineered by the British Army under the umbrella of post-war reparations – but its long-term success followed simply because it developed into a very good car for an emerging market.

It evolved without ever losing its focus or its essential identity. Crucially, and again as few might originally have imagined, it conquered America – even becoming an unlikely film star. In 1972 it overtook America's own pioneering "People's Car", the Ford Model T, as the biggest-selling car of all time. And it kept that title for a quarter of a century, before being overtaken in its turn in 1997 by the Toyota Corolla. Not that a 1997 Corolla had much more than the nameplate in common with the first 1966 Corolla – where a 1997 Beetle was unmistakably from the bloodline that had started even before World War II.

It was just as recognizable by the time it finally went out of production in 2003. Production and even evolution had survived in South America for another 25 years after the very last German-built Beetle (a cabriolet) left the line. By 30 July 2003, when the final car was completed in Puebla, Mexico, 21,529,464 Beetles had been built, every one clearly related.

Even before the final car was built, Volkswagen had launched the "New Beetle", based on a 1994 Concept Car, Concept 1. It evoked the classic Beetle, but other than in its modern interpretation of the classic shape, and popular as it became, it had no original Beetle DNA. That remains unique, and this is its story. •

brian laban

from humble beginnings

The original, classic Volkswagen Beetle finally went out of production in 2003, but the popular love affair with the Beetle continues to outlive the car, and shows little sign of fading. Against all odds, the car that grew out of a ground-breaking pre-war vision stayed in full-scale production for almost 60 years after the war ended. And during that time it became the most successful car ever built, smashing the production record set by Ford's legendary Model T by a huge margin, and holding that proud distinction for a quarter of a century, before being overtaken in its turn by a new generation of Japanese "world car". That the Beetle continues to win so many new admirers more than a decade after its first life has finally ended is a testimony to the timelessness of the original Porsche-inspired concept.

The story begins back in a politically unstable Germany of the 1930s, a country searching for an identity, a leader, a pride. With the arrival in German politics of a new figurehead by the name of Adolf Hitler, the scene was set for a major upheaval of all that had gone before. The impact of World War I had cost Germany dear, an expenditure of effort from which it would take years to recover. Gone, seemingly forever, were the days of an automobile industry dominated by luxury car manufacturers, for there was no longer a market for such vehicles. The German people, suffering from the effects of a declining economy, simply could no longer afford to buy luxury goods, let alone luxury cars.

For the man in the street, daily life meant walking or cycling to work, earning just enough money to keep his family, but little more. Some rode motorcycles, but few owned cars for they were too costly and, for most people, remained an unattainable dream. Hitler, however, had far grander plans for his countrymen than others before him. He envisaged a German workforce which travelled everywhere by car, along specially-built motorways, or *Autobahnen*.

His vision of a car for the People – a *Volksauto*, in the popular parlance of the time – was met with a certain reticence by most people involved in the contemporary automobile industry. After all, the likes of Horch, Adler and Daimler-Benz had each founded their reputations on grand luxury cars, not on low-cost four-seater economy vehicles.

Dr Ferdinand Porsche was one of just a few people who saw the merits of Hitler's vision as he, too, had been sketching ideas for a *Volksauto* while working with companies such as Zündapp and NSU. Hitler's proposals called for a car which could be sold for less than 1,000 Reichsmarks, a figure considered ludicrously low by most industrialists, although few had the courage to take the Führer to task on the matter. For Porsche, the figure was both an absurdity and a challenge.

With Hitler's support, Porsche's project reached fruition as the KdF-Wagen, or Strength-Through-Joy Car, the name being taken from the Nazi KdF socialist movement. An ingenious savings scheme was announced, whereby every worker could buy stamps, the value of which eventually added up to the cost of a new car – plus a few extras, such as compulsory insurance and delivery charges. Several thousand people signed up to join the scheme, but the outbreak of World War II brought about its downfall.

The story of the Volkswagen might have ended there, in 1939, but such was the soundness of Porsche's design that the car rose, phoenix-like, from the ashes of the Wolfsburg factory where it was assembled. The tale of its rebirth is one of the great legends of automobile history, the almost derelict factory being taken over by the British Army, which viewed it as a suitable location at which to repair worn-out military vehicles. Only when some of the officers, principal among them Major Ivan Hirst of the Royal Electrical and Mechanical Engineers, saw the potential offered by the Volkswagen, as it had become known, did production recommence.

By the time the Wolfsburg factory was handed back to the German people in 1949, the Volkswagen had proved its worth. In the hands of Heinz Nordhoff, the first post-war German head of the factory, sales of Porsche's dream car went from strength to strength. Sadly, Ferdinand Porsche himself was unable to witness the incredible success story which followed, a story which saw every sales and production record broken, worldwide. In 1951, illness, largely brought on by a period of post-war detention in France, was to claim the life of the man without whom there would have been no Volkswagen.

The full story of the amazing car which refused to die could not have been dreamed up by Hollywood: a financially unstable country led by an equally unstable dictator who dreams of a car for the masses. Enter a far-sighted engineer with a team of willing employees. Mix with a world war and stir in members of the British Army. The result: a world-beater in every sense.

The original Volkswagen also proved itself time and again to be one of life's great survivors. Over the years, there were many attempts to kill it off on the grounds that it was uneconomic to produce, too slow and poorly equipped for use in ever-more discerning markets, or for simply not being part of the grand plan as envisaged by the heads of a modern car-manufacturing empire. But for far longer than anyone could once have imagined, the Beetle simply refused to lie down and die. Even when production ended in Germany itself, for many years it continued unabated in South America – with Beetles being *imported* into Europe!

And even when the curtain finally came down on the real thing, Volkswagen's management clearly recognized the power of the name and the halo when they bestowed the title "New Beetle" to a new generation clearly designed to evoke the original.

But to fully understand how that car came into being, we need to start with the man who created it – Ferdinand Porsche.

The Birth Of The Dream

Make mention of the name Porsche in most circles and the first image that comes to mind is probably that of an exotic sports car built in Stuttgart. Few people outside the cognoscenti ever give thought to as humble a car as the Volkswagen Beetle when talking of such a name. Yet it was the same man, Dr Ferdinand Porsche, who was responsible for the production of both the People's Car and ultimately, under his own family name, such highly desirable sports cars as the 356 and the 911.

But the whole story begins a long, long time before that, as far back as the turn of the 20th century, which is when Porsche first turned his talents to car design.

Born on 3 September 1875 at Maffersdorf (then in Austria-Hungary and now known as Liberec in the Czech Republic), Ferdinand Porsche was the third son of a well-respected tinsmith, and soon joined his father as an apprentice to learn the skills of this worthy trade. However satisfying the prospect of carrying on the family business might have been to Ferdinand, he had his sights set far higher, for the end of the 19th century was a period when engineering technology was on the brink of expanding at an incredible rate. The young Porsche enrolled at the local technical college in Reichenberg and studied hard, soon developing a lasting interest in two relatively new areas of technology: domestic electricity and the internal combustion engine. Having witnessed the advantages of an efficient electrical supply first hand, while visiting the nearby Ginzkey's carpet factory, Porsche set about converting his parents' home to this new-found power source. He knew that both electricity and the combustion engine were going to prove of significant importance in the years ahead and absorbed as much information about them as he could find.

Despite his thirst for knowledge, Porsche was not an academic man in the truest sense, graduating from college with the lowest grades of his class. After their older brother Anton died following an industrial accident, Ferdinand's younger brother Oscar assumed the mantle of running the

family business and, with all such thoughts now firmly behind him, Porsche sought employment at Bela Egger's famous United Electrical Company at Fernkorngasse in Vienna, where he began his career sweeping floors and acting as a maintenance technician. However, his talents were soon recognized, and after just four years he was appointed manager of the test department where he was able to experiment with some of his own ideas.

Ironically, considering his poor academic grades at college, Porsche frequently sneaked secretly into lectures at the local university, where he was able to learn more about his favourite subjects. He began to sketch ideas for an electric car, a design which intrigued him, for he felt, quite rightly, that electrically-driven vehicles have much in their favour. For one thing, they are quiet and for another, they are totally without fumes. Only now, more than

a century later, are many of today's major car manufacturers beginning fully to exploit the benefits of such a concept. His first drawings were stolen, much to his fiancée Aloisia Kaes' fury, but this did not deter Ferdinand from continuing his work.

His first idea had been a highly intriguing design, whereby each wheel of a vehicle could be powered by its own electric motor fitted within the hub. The thinking behind this somewhat radical idea was that, at the time, almost all cars suffered from poor transmission design. Power losses were simply too great, while the output and reliability of contemporary internal combustion engines left much to be desired. Porsche developed his concept further and showed it to Ludwig Lohner, successor to his father Jacob as head of Jacob Lohner & Co, a well-established carriage builder in Vienna – in fact holding the distinction of "Coachbuilder to His Imperial Majesty".

Ludwig Lohner had himself already been investigating the possibility of offering an electrically-powered vehicle, feeling that the noisy and smelly internal combustion engine would probably not appeal to his more staid customers. However, although Lohner had a solid customer base and was an accomplished

Left For RM5 a week, workers could save for their own car. This pre-war brochure shows the *Sparkarte* savings card and the promised Kdf-Wagen.

carriage builder, his company lacked the technical expertise to produce the sort of vehicle he proposed. Porsche's designs and obvious talent were just what Lohner needed and, in 1898, he offered the young engineer a job as his designer.

Overnight Success

The result of this collaboration was the Lohner-Porsche Chaise, an electric vehicle with Porsche's beloved hub-drive motors, which proved capable of covering some 80km (50 miles) without recharging. The design so impressed Lohner that he asked Porsche to take the car to the 1900 Paris Universal Exposition where it was the subject of great interest, so much so that it was awarded a Grand Prize. At a time when motoring matters were dominating popular thinking, Porsche's success at the exposition made him famous overnight.

The next step was to develop a new vehicle which combined electric power with the internal combustion engine. A Daimler petrol engine was used to power generators which, In turn, supplied electricity to the hub-mounted motors. The car was an instant success, receiving much acclaim among many people in high society. The car, called the Mixte, proved to be popular, but it still did not satisfy Porsche – he had even more designs up his sleeve. Lohner, on the other hand, seemed quite content to concentrate on selling the

Mixte, having spent a large sum of money on its development costs. Porsche became restless and when, in 1905, he received an offer of employment from Austro-Daimler (or more correctly, Österreichische Daimler Motoren Werke as it then was), he readily accepted.

Within a year, Porsche was promoted to technical director and appointed to the board of the rather strait-laced company which was an offshoot of Daimler in Germany. There, he developed a car by the name of the Maja, a rather more conventional vehicle with a four-cylinder petrol engine and four-speed transmission. Even at this early stage in his professional life – Porsche was still only in his early thirties – he realized the value of success in competition as far as car sales were concerned. He entered three cars in the 1909 Prinz Heinrich endurance trial and all three won awards. The following year, Porsche entered an entirely new, streamlined car which earned itself the title of *Tulpenform*, or Tulip-shaped. Austro-Daimler cars won a total of 12 of the 17 test stages and took the first three prizes, the lead car driven by Ferdinand Porsche himself.

Military Matters

With the threat of war in Europe looming ever larger, Porsche found himself increasingly involved with designing aero-engines for Austro-Daimler. These impressive units,

each capable of producing over 300bhp yet weighing far less than their contemporary rivals, were used in both aircraft and dirigible airships. In 1913, he was called upon to design a tractor unit, capable of pulling an immense mortar developed by Skoda for the military. His design was based upon the principle of petrol/electrical power first used in the Mixte car for Lohner. It almost goes without saying that the design was a success and saw regular action throughout World War I.

However, the war ended in defeat for the German Empire and triggered the consequent collapse of its financial fortunes. At a stroke, there was little or no demand for the fine vehicles which Porsche had been responsible for designing while employed with Lohner and Austro-Daimler. However, Porsche was not one to look on the black side. Instead he realized there would soon be a demand for an inexpensive family car, capable of echoing the role pioneered by Ford's legendary Model T in America. Others in his company were not so convinced, feeling that Austro-Daimler should continue to build the large, quality limousines for which it was famous. Even when the company received a commission to build a small, lightweight sports car for competition use – subsequently called the Sascha – the directors showed no enthusiasm. Again Porsche's design was a success, but Austro-Daimler refused to make more funds available to develop it.

Ultimately, after an explosive meeting with the company's financiers, Porsche stormed out.

The German Daimler concern was quick to make him an offer, and Porsche was appointed to the position of technical director and became a member of the board at the Stuttgart factory. His blunt manner did not always go down well with the somewhat conservative Daimler management, but he soon earned the respect of his workforce. He proceeded to design a number of impressive vehicles under Daimler's prestigious Mercedes name, several of which were to become legends in their own lifetimes, such as the mighty SS and SSK models with their thundering supercharged engines.

Troubled Times

However, Porsche still longed to be able to push forward his idea for a car for the masses, but once again met with resistance from his employers. Ironically, one of the reasons why his pleas were met with indifference was that, as the economy was in decline, Daimler felt it should concentrate on building only profitable models. To Daimler, that meant large, luxury vehicles, not small, low-cost family cars. Once again, a disagreement with management saw Porsche's departure from Stuttgart, this time following the merger that created Daimler-Benz AG in 1926. With more than a hint of irony, the alleged cause of the disagreement was over the reliability of a new small car called the Stuttgart!

Porsche was immediately offered a position at Steyr, in Vienna, and in 1929 he found himself heading for his homeland. At Steyr, he was responsible for the design of two successful cars, a small saloon very much along the lines of Daimler's Stuttgart model, and a larger limousine, called the Austria. Both were fine vehicles and met with much acclaim, especially when displayed at the 1929 Paris Motor Show. However, Porsche's euphoria was short-lived, for Steyr collapsed and the company's affairs were, coincidentally, handed over to the same financiers who handled Austro-Daimler. With his enthusiasm for car manufacturing at an all-time low, Ferdinand Porsche turned his back on further employment within the car industry and headed for Stuttgart once more to open a design studio, Dr Ing hc Ferdinand Porsche GmbH, Konstruktionsbüro für Motoren- und Fahrzeugbau – the Porsche Bureau – through which he could offer his services to industry as an engineering consultant. The company registration date was 1 January 1931.

Torsion Bars

The new bureau's first client was the Wanderer Auto Company, although Porsche didn't want Wanderer (or anyone else) thinking they actually *were* the first, so his first design for them was labelled Project 7. It was one of a pair of cars that Porsche designed for Wanderer, albeit neither being the "People's Car" which he so longed to build. However, he did incorporate at least one design idea which he had been considering for some time: torsion bar suspension. Porsche had long felt that the days of the traditional leaf spring were numbered, especially since it was very difficult to achieve the correct spring rate, and hence an acceptable ride quality, when using such a suspension medium on a lightweight vehicle. Porsche's torsion system consisted of a bar, one end of which was held solidly in the chassis, the other end being connected to the wheels which caused it to twist as the suspension rose and fell over rough ground. There were two major advantages to this design: torsion bar suspension is very compact (and thus lends itself to use on a small car) and it displays a rising spring rate, i.e., the more the suspension is deflected, the stiffer it becomes.

So, some of the elements of the future Beetle were starting to come together: a downturn in the German economy, Porsche's long-held dream for a small car, and now the ideal suspension system. What was missing was a company prepared to give Porsche his head. But one tempting offer was to come from an unlikely source.

In 1932, Ferdinand was approached by a Soviet engineering delegation, who wished to offer him the opportunity to emigrate to the USSR and become a state-sponsored industrial designer. The offer *was* extremely tempting, for the Soviets offered Porsche everything he could want, including a new home for his wife and family, a blank development cheque and the possibility of starting work on a small car for the masses. However, despite a visit to the USSR which left him very impressed, Porsche felt that he could not bring himself to turn his back on his homeland and the team he had built up around him.

Back in his design bureau, Porsche had also found himself in contact with Fritz Neumeyer, head of the Zündapp motorcycle company in Nürnberg. Neumeyer, like Porsche, believed that the time was right for the introduction of a small car – a *kleinauto* – which would appeal to the person who wished to progress from riding a motorcycle to owning a family car. Indeed, Zündapp had even been sketching some ideas of its own.

Project No 12

For Ferdinand Porsche, the whole concept of a car for the people had become something of an obsession. He devoted much time and effort, and his own money, to designing a small car of revolutionary layout. The design, known as Project No 12, was a strange-looking vehicle with a sloping nose, curved rear bodywork and a rear-mounted engine. The reason for the latter configuration was to provide better traction on indifferent road surfaces, something that may have been a problem due to the vehicle's low weight. Naturally, Porsche's beloved torsion bar suspension was also part of the plan.

Perhaps the most technically intriguing part of the design was the engine that Porsche himself proposed: a peculiar three-cylinder unit with the cylinders mounted radially about the crankshaft, rather like an aircraft engine. Air-cooling helped keep both the cost and the weight to a minimum. Also worthy of note was the lack of a conventional chassis. Porsche's work on aircraft design had led him to appreciate the quite considerable weight benefits that could be had by careful strengthening of what might otherwise appear to be a rather weak design. A flat, sheet metal pan with a central backbone member was made more rigid by the clever use of small, but effective, ribs pressed into the metalwork.

After three months devoted to perfecting the design on paper, Porsche was forced to consider putting the whole project on hold as he was fast running out of money. However, despite the indifference shown by others in the industry to Project No 12, Fritz Neumeyer heard of the design, asked to see the drawings and liked what he saw. Porsche was given the go-ahead to develop the concept as far as building three running prototypes. However, there was to be one major alteration: the engine should be a five-cylinder, water-cooled design of radial layout, which had always been Zündapp's preference. Porsche was not enthusiastic but agreed to make the change. It was to prove a mistake as these first cars were terribly unreliable, their engines seizing almost immediately. To add to the problem, Porsche's innovative suspension system proved troublesome, with the torsion bars snapping with frustrating regularity.

Neumeyer became downhearted with the whole situation and rapidly lost interest, preferring instead to concentrate on building motorcycles. Porsche was thanked for his efforts, paid a sum of money and given one of the prototypes to take away. It is worth noting that this car continued in regular use until 1944, when it is believed to have been destroyed in an air-raid on the Wolfsburg factory. Needless to say, Porsche was disappointed at the outcome of Project No 12. It was a classic case of so-near-yet-so-far.

However, hope was in sight when Fritz von Falkenhayn, head of the NSU company, let it be known that his company was interested in developing a *Volksauto*, or People's Car. Porsche once more rose to the challenge and produced another prototype – Project No 32. This was similar to its Zündapp predecessor, but more refined in its overall appearance.

The headlamps, for example, were incorporated into the front wings and the whole body shape was more graceful. The greatest improvement, as far as Porsche was concerned, was the adoption of an air-cooled engine, this time a four-cylinder, horizontally-opposed design, not unlike the aero engines he had designed for Austro-Daimler.

A total of three prototypes were built and each proved to be a success, despite continuing problems with the torsion-bar suspension. The cause of the breakages was discovered to be a matter of incorrect heat treatment of the metal, not one of a flawed basic concept. Von Falkenhayn was delighted with the cars, being especially impressed by the performance, and gave his approval to further development of the *Volksauto*.

The Rise Of Hitler

However, history was about to be made in German political circles when, on 30 January 1933, an ambitious Adolf Hitler was appointed Chancellor of Germany by von Hindenburg, the President. Hitler, head of the German National Socialist Workers' (or Nazi) party, was an unashamed car enthusiast. Indeed, ten years earlier he had spent the last of his party's funds on buying himself an expensive Mercedes-Benz for "official purposes". His first official engagement was to open the 1933 Berlin Motor Show, where he took the opportunity to speak out about his grand plan to motorize Germany, building a network of motorways – or *autobahnen* – along which the German people could travel in their very own cars. Quite what inspired Hitler to have this vision is unclear – his own love was for powerful,

Right The Zündapp Type 12 took to the road in 1932. It was derived from Porsche's Project No 12.

high-performance cars, even though he never himself learned to drive. Possibly the idea came to him while he was in prison, some ten years earlier, where he read a copy of Henry Ford's autobiography. Ford's writings captivated the young Hitler, with their tales of mass production and cheap motoring – or maybe it was simply the fact that Ford was known to hold anti-Semitic views that appealed to Hitler's imagination.

Whatever the reason behind it, Hitler's speech sent shock waves through the German car industry, for few of the larger, well-established manufacturers had shown any interest in a *Volksauto*, as Porsche was only too well aware. At the time he was working with NSU on Project No 32, and also with Auto-Union on the design of a radical new racing car, intended to take on the might of Mercedes-Benz on the racetracks of Europe. As Mercedes had been given a government subsidy by Hitler, Porsche argued that Auto-Union deserved the same. Hitler disagreed, feeling that Germany only needed one outstanding car in order to beat foreign rivals. Porsche argued long and hard, laying out the proposed technical specification of the Auto-Union: a mid-mounted V16 engine, torsion-bar suspension with trailing arms at the front, swing axles at the rear, and an impressive streamlined body. By the end of his outburst, Porsche had convinced Hitler of his argument and a subsidy was made available to Auto-Union. The result

was a series of race cars which not only beat the Mercedes-Benz team cars on a regular basis but also dominated Grand Prix racing in Europe. And they were reputed to be capable of speeds close to 322km/h (200mph) in a straight line.

Towards the end of the year, von Falkenhayn was forced to pull out of the *Volksauto* project, largely due to a long-standing agreement between NSU and Fiat which forbade NSU from becoming involved with car manufacture. Porsche was devastated by the news, for it must have seemed to him that he would never find a supporter for his much-loved concept. However, a chance meeting with Jakob Werlin, a Berlin Mercedes-Benz dealer and close confidant of Hitler, gave him the opportunity to discuss his plans once again. Werlin listened to Porsche with interest, knowing full well that Hitler was anxious to see such a car take to the roads. Porsche had already composed a lengthy paper on the subject and sent it to the German transport ministry, and it is almost certain that Hitler, being such a car buff, would have heard of its existence.

In January 1934, Hitler once again addressed the crowds at the Berlin Motor Show, talking further of his wish for a car for the people – the difference this year was that by now he had been appointed Führer (leader) of the Nazi party and his words had far more political clout than they had 12 months earlier. Shortly afterwards, he asked to meet Ferdinand Porsche

to discuss their individual ideas. They found they had much in common, not only in terms of car-related topics, but also in their background, for Hitler had also been born in the backwoods of Austro-Hungary. The two discussed at length their ideas for a small car, Hitler listening intently to Porsche's plans. These called for a car that weighed approximately 650kg (1,435lb), could travel at 100km/h (62mph) and used an air-cooled engine capable of producing around 26 horsepower. Hitler agreed that the engine should be air-cooled, but added that the car should be able to travel 100km for every seven litres of fuel (40mpg) and cruise at, not just reach, a speed of 100km/h (62mph). On the subject of cost, Porsche felt at this early stage that such a car could be built for around RM (Reichsmark) 1,550.

The Volksauto

Hitler was excited about the project and ordered the RDA (*Reichsverband der Deutschen Automobilindustrie*, or German motor industry association) to proceed with the scheme. The RDA was to work with Porsche and a contract was drawn up which held two surprises for the designer: the time allocated to build three prototypes was to be ten months, not one year as Porsche had initially hoped, and the cost would be no more than RM900! Porsche thought Hitler must be mad on both accounts, but looked upon the whole thing

as a challenge that he would try to meet. The RDA called on the rest of the car industry to become involved with the project, but there was little enthusiasm for the scheme. Most thought it impractical, while others resented the involvement of Porsche, evidently jealous of his seemingly close relationship with Hitler. If the truth be known, the relationship extended no further than a common love of the concept of a *Volksauto* – Porsche had no political aspirations and never showed any enthusiasm for Nazi principles.

As there was little support from the rest of the industry, Porsche took it upon himself and his team to build the *Volksauto* prototypes at his Stuttgart garage. After ten months of hard work, the vehicles were still not ready and, at the 1935 Berlin Motor Show, Hitler was forced to make a speech that was, to those in the know, an exercise in stalling for time. He promised testing of the prototypes by mid-year, although Porsche knew this would not be possible. However, Hitler was not one to lose face and he remained up-beat and confident about the whole project.

By the end of the year, two prototypes were completed, but Porsche requested permission to build a third, the request being granted now that it was realized that the original timetable had been unworkable. The first two prototypes, one a saloon (V1), the other a convertible (V2), featured aluminium bodies formed over a wooden frame, while another series of three cars of the same design (VW3) were all saloons with steel bodies. As far as the engine was concerned, Porsche favoured the idea of using a two-stroke design, as it was both efficient and inexpensive to build. However, testing soon showed that the design was unsuited to the chosen purpose and he finally settled on a four-cylinder, horizontally-opposed, four-stroke 985cc unit designed by Franz Reimspiess.

The matter of cost remained a bugbear for Porsche and, indeed, for the rest of the industry. The manufacturer Opel was so sure that the project was doomed to failure that its leader, Wilhelm von Opel, suggested to Porsche that he had worked things rather nicely to his own advantage: "It's a wonderful contract, Herr Porsche. Ten months on good pay and then you tell your leaders their project is impossible". The head of BMW considered the whole idea of an inexpensive car a waste of time, suggesting with patrician hauteur that the working classes would be perfectly happy to travel everywhere by bus!

Testing Times

Also concerned about how the final product could be put into full-scale production, Porsche visited manufacturing plants in the USA (including Ford in Dearborn) to see for himself how the latest mass-production techniques could be employed in Germany. He was impressed by what he saw there, but less so when he visited the Austin factory, at Longbridge, in England. There, he felt, the factory was old and inefficient, with the production lines working at a snail's pace compared with their American counterparts.

It was not until 12 October 1936, that the three VW Series 3 (or VW3) prototypes were eventually turned over to the RDA for testing, well over 18 months late. The first two cars had already been driven extensively by the Porsche team, one car having covered 800km (500 miles), the second almost 4,800km (3,000 miles). The third car was delivered directly to the RDA. The cars were immediately subjected to a rigorous test schedule, which called for them to cover a total of 48,000km (30,000 miles) each, on all kinds of roads under all weather conditions. They were to be driven for 800km (500 miles) a day, six days a week until the test programme was complete.

As the cars had been assembled under less than perfect conditions, with little or no opportunity to test materials or achieve accurate machining tolerances, failures of some kind had to be expected. Indeed, there were several members of the RDA who must have secretly hoped the whole project would prove to be abortive. Under the watchful eye of Wilhelm Vorwig, the RDA's project manager, the test programme went ahead in earnest and it was not long before teething troubles made their presence felt.

One car suffered problems with the front wheel bearings, burned out its valves and then suffered brake failure on two occasions. All three cars suffered from broken crankshafts so regularly that the stock of spares was soon used up. Daimler-Benz cast some more but they too broke. It was only when replacement crankshafts were forged rather than cast that the problem was effectively solved.

The final outcome of this programme was a report, penned by Vorwig, which pronounced the basic design to be sound. Despite his association with the RDA, and therefore almost rival sympathies, Vorwig was forced to concede that there were few flaws in the overall concept. The many failures that had been experienced during the test period could be attributed to the fact that the cars had been built under less than favourable conditions, using materials that were frequently of imperfect quality. No part of the report, other than the matter of price, struck a negative chord as far as Hitler was concerned – the RDA was still of the opinion that the car could not be built as cheaply as the Führer had hoped.

The go-ahead was given to build a further series of 30 prototypes (VW30) which were to be test driven by some 200 army drivers, accompanied by uniformed SS officers to keep an eye on things. The extensive test schedule called for each car to cover 80,000km (50,000 miles), with the drivers showing the cars no mercy. Indeed, the army personnel had been chosen specifically, as their lack of mechanical sympathy was most likely to imitate that of the average German worker who had probably never even driven a car before. The cars passed this new test with flying colours, although the maximum speed of 100km/h (62mph) proved to be a little difficult to attain at times. Only when an alternative 1131cc prototype engine was tried did the performance significantly improve.

A further series of 44 cars – the VW38 – was built in 1937, with several detail changes made to the design and engine construction to take into account the lessons learnt by the VW30 test programme. The new car was virtually identical to the eventual production version and included such additions as a pair of D-shaped rear windows (previous prototypes had none), front-hinged doors as opposed to rear-hinged "suicide" doors and running-boards between the front and rear wings. Mechanically, the VW38 used the 985cc engine seen in the VW30, which produced 24bhp and had a bore and stroke of 70mm x 64mm (2.75in x 2.52in). The four-speed transmission was of a transaxle design, whereby the final drive

Left Some of the Type 30 prototypes ready for road testing in 1937.

unit was incorporated within the same casing as the gear cluster itself. With Porsche's beloved torsion-bar suspension, the car had a kerb weight of 750kg (1,654lb), some 100kg (220lb) more than had originally been hoped. However, despite this weight gain, the VW38, and its immediate pre-production successor the VW39, were capable of reaching – and maintaining – a cruising speed of 100km/h (62mph).

The matter of how and where the new car – by now referred to by everybody as the Volkswagen or People's Car – would be produced had remained as much a mystery to Porsche as it did to most others involved in the project. It became obvious that there could be only one satisfactory solution and that was to build a new factory from the ground up on what is known today as a "green field site". A search was made to find the ideal location; it should be near a canal or river to allow the easy transport of raw materials, and close to a source of labour. Eventually the 14th-century estate of Count von Schulenburg, Schloss Wolfsburg at Fallersleben, was chosen, although it has to be said that the Count had very little say in the matter. Von Schulenburg was outraged at the idea of having to hand over a proportion of his land and protested at the highest level, but to no avail. Unfortunately, because of the proximity of the Mittelland Canal to this estate, the Fallersleben site seemed perfect.

Right Hitler accepts a birthday gift of a convertible from Ferdinand Porsche, Berlin, April 1939.

KdF-Stadt

Hitler appointed a young architect by the name of Peter Koller to design the new factory, and its construction was overseen by Robert Ley, chief of the Nazi Party Labour Organization. Heeding lessons learned during Porsche's visits to the USA (a second visit had been made largely in an effort to tempt expatriate German technicians to return to their homeland), the new factory was built to the highest standards and followed the latest designs employed by the leading American manufacturers of the time.

On 26 May 1938, the cornerstone of the new factory was laid as part of a grand ceremony, in which Adolf Hitler made a rousing speech outlining his plans for the future. In it he referred to the new car not as the Volkswagen but as the KdF-Wagen – literally, the Strength Through Joy car. The KdF (*Kraft durch Freude*) movement was Hitler's own brainchild, conceived to motivate the German people by giving them a sense of purpose, promising them cheap housing, holidays, and, of course, low-cost motoring. The new town built to provide housing for the workforce would be called the KdF-Stadt. He also announced a revolutionary plan to allow the low-paid workers to buy their own

KdF-Wagen. This scheme was clever, of that there is no doubt, for it offered potential customers the opportunity to buy weekly savings stamps at RM5 each.

A total of 50 stamps filled each book and the total cost of each car was set at RM990. However, on top of this was a RM50 delivery charge and RM200 for a two-year compulsory insurance scheme. Considering that the average worker's wage was little more than RM200–300 per month, the car was not quite the bargain it may have first seemed. Despite that, no fewer than 336,638 people signed up for the scheme, providing the government with no less than RM268 million income.

Naturally, this savings card (*Sparkarte*) scheme was like a gift from God as far as the KdF programme was concerned, for not

only did it provide money up front for the whole project, but it also amounted to the best possible market research anyone could wish for. For example, there were three different versions of the KdF-Wagen on offer: a regular saloon, a sunroof model and a cabriolet. When they opened their savings accounts, the workers had to state which model they eventually wanted to take delivery of, this form of subscription naturally giving the factory a clear indication of how many of each it would need to build. It is interesting to note that the majority of people chose to pay the extra RM60 for the optional sunroof model. What is more distressing is that not one of those 336,638 people ever took delivery of their KdF-Wagen under the savings scheme. The outbreak of World War II in September 1939 would see to that.●

the phoenix rises

As far back as 1938, there were moves afoot to produce a military version of what became known as the KdF-Wagen. In fact, early in January of that year, the head of the SS test team, Hauptsturmführer Liese, received a directive that a military version of the VW30 prototype should be prepared, to see if there was any future for such a car. Working to strict guidelines laid down by the Wehrmacht – which called for all military vehicles to have a minimum power output of 25bhp, to weigh no more than 950kg (2,094lb), including 400kg (882lb) for men and weaponry, and have a ground clearance of at least 240mm (9.5in) – Porsche began to investigate the suitability of his beloved People's Car for military use. In November of that year, another version was built, based this time on the much-improved VW38 saloon. The result was a far superior vehicle which clearly demonstrated that the concept was worth pursuing. This VW38 variation, the first version of the Porsche Type 62, was equipped with curvaceous open bodywork but no doors – simple canvas flaps provided weather protection when needed. Mechanically, the vehicle was unchanged from its civilian counterpart, the 985cc, flat-four, air-cooled engine providing all the power necessary for such a lightweight machine.

In 1939, a revised prototype was displayed at the Vienna Fair still with the designation Type 62 (or VW62).

This was the result of a collaboration between Porsche and the Trutz coachworks in Gotha, a company well versed in building military machinery. This version of the Type 62 was a simple, slab-sided vehicle with a sharply sloping front and an abruptly cut-off back, separate wings and a crude but well-proportioned canvas hood. In tests, the Type 62 (in either body variation) acquitted itself well, the light weight and rear-mounted engine allowing the Porsche-designed prototype to cope with slippery conditions with ease. However, the inadequate ground clearance remained a problem and prevented the vehicle from gaining acceptance in military circles – it simply could not cope with any kind of rough terrain. Porsche tried fitting 18in diameter wheels in place of the regular 16in design, but that did little to help, so it was back to the drawing board.

Kübelwagen

The result was the Type 82, a vehicle similar in style to the Type 62 but with one major improvement: far greater ground clearance. This was achieved, at the front, by relocating the stub axles further down the steering knuckle and, at the back, by the addition of a pair of reduction boxes, one at the end of each rear axle. The result was an increase in ground clearance from 220mm to 290mm (8.6in to 11.4in) at a stroke. Adding these reduction boxes solved another problem – the design brief called for a vehicle which could be driven at the walking pace of a soldier carrying a backpack. This was judged to be 4km/h (2.5mph) but, with standard gearing, the slowest a Type 62 could be driven was 8km/h (5mph). Reduction boxes allowed the overall gearing to be lowered still further and thus another problem was solved. Even with two-wheel drive, the Type 82 became an accomplished off-road vehicle, thanks to the addition of a simple limited-slip differential system. Unfortunately, this was to prove troublesome and unreliable and it took a further two years of development in the field finally to cure the problems.

Production began in earnest in 1940, with the chassis and drivetrain assembled in KdF-Stadt and the bodies by the American-owned Ambi-Budd company in Berlin. Partly due to its bucket-style seating (*Kübelsitz*) and partly due to its shape, the new vehicle soon earned itself the nickname of *Kübelwagen* or, literally, "bucket-car". The term was, however, one of affection, for the Type 82 rapidly established itself as the mainstay of the German military, proving to be a match for the seemingly more sophisticated US-designed General Purpose Vehicle, or Jeep. With its air-cooled engine, the Kübelwagen was equally at home in the biting cold of the Russian Front or in the desert heat of North Africa.

A Life Saver

Field-Marshal Rommel, the "Desert Fox", became a great fan of the Kübelwagen and even claimed that it had saved his life. One day, his driver strayed into a minefield, but the light weight of the vehicle prevented it from detonating any mines, although the heavier vehicle following behind was blown up and its occupants killed. Considering the versatility of the design, it is perhaps slightly ironic that, due to a bureaucratic mix up, a series of 500 Kübelwagens specially adapted for use in the desert found their way to the Russian Front. They performed well under the extreme conditions, however, as did the 500 Russian-bound Kübels that Rommel received by default.

Strictly speaking, with its modest power output, the Type 82 fell short of German military requirements, but this fact was overlooked once it had been shown that the basic design was so effective. In 1943, however, the engine was redesigned with a larger cylinder bore (75mm/2.9in instead of 70mm/2.75in), which resulted in a capacity of 1,131cc and a slightly increased power output of just 25bhp, sufficient to silence any critics who might have complained about the original Type 82 not meeting the required standards.

Shortly after the Kübelwagen went into production, work began on

developing an amphibious version. The project was given the factory designation Type 128 and resulted in a tub-like vehicle based on Type 82 components but with the added advantage of four-wheel drive to cope with poor terrain. The first prototype, based on a modified Kübelwagen, was put to the test in July 1940 and served to prove that, once again, Porsche's basic design was sound. By the end of September that year, a number of hand-built prototypes had undergone extensive testing in the Max-Eyth-See near Stuttgart, these having more rounded bodywork with a hull-like lower half.

Mechanically, the Type 128 shared the same engine and basic transmission as its forbears, but drive was taken from the front of the transaxle forward to a separate differential unit mounted adjacent to the front axle beam. Two drive shafts

with universal joints transmitted power to the front wheels while, at both ends of the vehicle, rubber seals prevented the ingress of water into either the interior or the engine bay. Both differential units were equipped with a limited slip system and an extra, cross-country, ratio was added to the gearbox. The Type 128 could be driven in either two- or four-wheel-drive modes, the selection being made by the same lever which selected cross-country gearing.

To provide motive power when in the amphibious mode, a propeller was fitted to the rear of the Type 128, with the drive being taken from the end of the crankshaft. In normal on-road use, the propeller was hinged up out of the way but it could be swung down into position when the vehicle entered the water. It is interesting to note that the rear wheels continued to turn in the water, helping forward motion, and that the front wheels were used to steer – an indicator on the dashboard showed their position. Capable of just 10km/h (6mph) in water, the heavy (at 900kg/1,985lb) Type 128 could still manage 80km/h (50mph) on dry land. If this amphibious machine had one failing, it was that it was too bulky, the wheelbase remaining the same as the KdF-Wagen's at 2,400mm (94.5in).

Schwimmwagen

Ferry Porsche, Ferdinand's son who had worked alongside his father since 1931, later recalled a visit from a Waffen SS delegation, during which he was asked if it would be possible to fit a Volkswagen engine into a motorcycle. Ferry pointed out that his father's company did

not design motorcycles but asked what the problem was. It turned out that the SS was after an all-terrain vehicle which could cope with everything from hard ground to soft mud and slime. Such a vehicle needed to be lightweight and compact. The young Porsche suggested that he might be able to help, and the design team returned to their office in April 1941 to come up with the Type 166. This was not a motorcycle but another four-wheeled amphibious vehicle developed as a result of lessons learned from the Type 128, this time with a narrower track and a wheelbase which was some 400mm (15.75in) less than that of its predecessor, making it far more manoeuvrable. By August, a prototype was ready for testing and it proved successful, the reduced size and 10kg (22lb) lower weight

meeting the SS's brief perfectly.

The Type 166, or Schwimmwagen as it became known, proved to be hugely popular with the German Army, seeing action on all fronts. Its primary role was that of a reconnaissance vehicle, as its superb off-road capabilities allowed it to tackle terrain that no other vehicle could cope with. In most instances, it proved even more capable than a motorcycle. In total, 14,283 examples were built between 1942, when they first went into production, and 1944 when a shortage of raw materials brought things to a standstill.

Several other variations on the Type 82 theme appeared on Porsche's drawing board during the war, some of which were quite bizarre, such as the Type 155, a half-track Kübelwagen, and the Type 157 – a model designed to run along railway tracks. Other versions included those converted to accept twin rear wheels for better traction, radio cars, fire tenders and munitions carriers. However, two of the more practical were the Type 82E and the Type 877 (often referred to simply, but incorrectly, as the Type 87). The former was essentially a KdF-Wagen bodyshell mounted on a regular two-wheel-drive Kübelwagen chassis, the greater ride height giving the vehicle better cross-country capabilities while retaining the practicality of

an enclosed saloon car. The Type 87 was in fact a four-wheel-drive version of the regular Kübelwagen, but the designation has popularly become associated with what is more correctly known as the Type 877 – this was a KdF-Wagen saloon bodyshell on the running gear of the Type 128, four-wheel-drive amphibious vehicle.

Kommandeurwagen

Known as the Kommandeurwagen, the Type 877 was only built in small numbers – just 667 were built between 1942 and 1944 – and, on paper at least, it clearly showed promise. However, these four-wheel-drive saloons were not easy cars to drive, for the ratios in the front and rear differentials were not the same. Today, it is not uncommon to find four-wheel-drive vehicles in which different amounts of torque are applied to the front and rear wheels, but that is achieved by such technology as centre differentials, viscous couplings and the like. With no such technical delights available at the time, the Type 877 relied upon a certain amount of slippage on loose surfaces to prevent the drivetrain from tying itself in knots. The steering was heavy and vague, lacking any sensation of self-centring due to the four-wheel-drive conversion. Even

Left The Type 64 (also referred to as the K-10) was one of three vehicles built to contest the planned Berlin to Rome road race of 1939. The outbreak of war meant the event did not take place, but the Type 64 showed clear hints of Porsche-designed sports cars to come.

on smooth road surfaces, the Type 877 tended to weave its way down the road. It also has to be said that the sound generated by the complex transmission system was enough to drown out even that generated by the noisy air-cooled engine. With a full payload, the Type 877 weighed in at a massively overweight 1,240kg (2,734lb) – more than enough for the poor 25bhp engine.

But what of the basic KdF-Wagen saloon? As explained at the end of the first chapter, not one of the German workers who signed up for the *Sparkarte* scheme ever received their cars, although a fair proportion of them actually paid for the car in full. So was it all a giant fraud? Probably not, for the money paid into the KdF savings scheme was kept in a special account in Berlin and was found to be untouched after the war. Sadly, the money was seized by the Soviet forces and was never seen again. Up until August 1940, a total of 54 KdF saloons had been built, along with six cabriolets. All were destined for testing purposes or use by high-ranking officials. It is worthy of note that few of these officials ever appeared to use their KdF-Wagens, preferring to be seen in their more glamorous Mercedes.

Official production commenced on 11 July 1941, somewhat late in the day to be of any use to the workers. The first cars were delivered on 3 September and, by the time production finally ceased, on 7 August 1944, some 630 saloons

and a further 13 cabriolets had been built, again principally for use by the military or other government departments, although some remained at the factory for use by the staff.

Throughout this period, the matter of model designation has grown to become something of a nightmare as far as the historian is concerned, for it would appear that the same model might be given two different design numbers, while two others might share the same designation. It is, therefore, worth taking a look at what appears to be a contradictory puzzle. The original Project numbers used by Porsche related directly to the chronology of the various projects, hence Project No 7, the first Wanderer (rather than the non-existent Project No 1, as explained in the previous chapter) was the first, the lack of a Project 11 making No 12 the fifth, etc. It really *was* complicated. In VW terms, the first recognizable prototypes of the People's Car were the V1, V2 and V3 models, of which the latter appeared in three guises: V3-I, V3-II and V3-III. Next in line was the VW30, the series of 30 vehicles as tested by the SS, followed by the VW38 and VW39, whose numbers appear to relate more to the year of construction rather than any project number or quantity.

When the first pre-production KdF-Wagen was built, it was given the Porsche designation Type 60, with a series of "K" number suffixes used to differentiate between

differing body styles. Amongst these was the K-1 saloon, K-8 saloon with sunroof, K-9, the convertible KdF-Wagen, and the K-10, a series of three Type 60-based sports cars built by Porsche to contest the 1939 Berlin–Rome road race (also known as the Type 64!). There was even a K-11 which was to be a plastic-bodied version intended to side-step future material shortages.

After Type 60 came a whole host of variations, many of which progressed no further than the drawing board. A right-hand-drive model (Type 66) was even considered, as was an invalid carriage conversion (Type 67).

The potential confusion deepens when some models were allocated new numbers, such as the Type 92 (the cross-country SS version of the Type 82E) which later became known as the Type 51! As we have seen, the Type 87 was a four-wheel-drive Type 82, the Kommandeurwagen, but that designation was also popularly applied to the Type 877, the four-wheel-drive KdF-Wagen. After the war, the designations became even more convoluted, with the Type 82 Kübelwagen becoming known as the Type 21, the Type 60 saloon becoming the Type 11 and ultimately the Type 1.

Among the considerable number of Porsche design numbers can be seen the Type 230 (VW with gas generator), Type 330 (VW saloon with combined wood/gas fuel system), Type 331 (VW with "native"

fuel system) and the Type 332 (VW with anthracite coal system). These were some of the last of the wartime designs and took heed of the fact that liquid fuels were all but unobtainable. Several of these unlikely vehicles were built, in both saloon and Kübelwagen form, the conversion equipment being extremely ungainly and adding considerably to the all-up weight. Filled with coal, for instance, the Type 332 weighed some 80kg (176lb) more than the basic Type 82.

Wolfsburg Is Born

Such designs were a barometer of the way the war was going for Germany: fuel shortages and a serious lack of raw materials, along with ever-intensifying air-raids, made it clear that the end was in sight. As far as the factory was concerned, it came on 10/11 April 1945, when advancing American troops finally appeared on the horizon. They halted some 10km (6 miles) short of the factory for the simple reason that their maps did not even show the town, KdF-Stadt, to exist. The occupants of the town, and workers at the factory, were keen to make contact with the Americans, preferring to place themselves in their hands rather than those of the Soviet Army, which was also approaching them.

A delegation from the town made its way perilously through the countryside, which was thick with marauding Russian troops and the remnants of SS regiments keen on seeking revenge against anyone who stood in their way. The American troops were bemused to find themselves being begged by German citizens to take them prisoner and take over their town, but then many of the workers at the factory were either people who had lived in the USA before the war or were forced labourers who feared reprisals from the SS. At this time the town had no "civilian" name. Prior to and throughout the war, it had been referred to as KdF-Stadt, but the cessation of hostilities meant that the KdF movement no longer existed. A new title was called for and a meeting of the town council in May 1945, held under the jurisdiction of the British, resulted in the Wolfsburg name being adopted, it being taken from the nearby castle, Schloss Wolfsburg. The factory was in a bad way, with two thirds of the buildings having been either destroyed or severely damaged by Allied bombing raids, and many locals felt it unlikely that production would ever recommence.

Immediately after the war, Germany was split into sectors, each coming under the control of one or other of the Allied forces. Wolfsburg, being well off the beaten track, was not initially paid much heed and found itself under British control. Only later did the Soviets realize how important the site could be and show any interest. Following almost six long years of war, there was a desperate need for a vehicle

repair facility, as the Allied lorries and Jeeps were by now worn beyond further use. Under MilGov (Military Government) command, Colonel Michael McEvoy was given the task of looking after vehicle repair. He had, quite by chance, driven a KdF-Wagen in 1938 while he was working with Mercedes-Benz. McEvoy, then, above all others, was quick to appreciate the worth of what he found at Wolfsburg. He quickly established a working party of REME (Royal Electrical and Mechanical Engineers) personnel to take a close look at the remains of the factory to investigate what could and could not be of use. In August 1945, Major Ivan Hirst, also of REME, was placed in control of the situation and a full appraisal of the factory was made.

Amid The Ruins

Among the ruins, there were several uncompleted Kübelwagens and many spares. It was not long before some of these vehicles were built up and put to use, their performance meeting with universal approval. However, the problem as far as production of any wholly new Kübels was concerned was that the originally American-owned Ambi-Budd factory in Berlin, which had produced the bodies for the factory, was now in the hands of Soviet troops. The press tooling had most likely been destroyed in Allied air raids – if not, then it was unlikely that the new owners would release it for anyone else to use.

Hirst was generally impressed with the basic design of the car, and thought that it might have a future. He looked around and rescued from the ruins machinery that had been used in production, and set about finding still more which had been dispersed to various sites in the area. With this machinery, essential work was carried out to the old army vehicles which had been sent to Wolfsburg for repair. Hirst also managed to get one or two KdF saloons up and running, painting one of them khaki green and sending it off to British Army headquarters for appraisal. Much to his surprise, an order for some 20,000 vehicles came back by return. Even the Americans, French and Soviets expressed an interest in acquiring some examples.

Had the Kübelwagen tooling not been lost, the simplest solution would have been to build new versions of the Type 82, but instead Hirst had to consider assembling the Type 60 (KdF saloon) instead. The press shop at Wolfsburg had been damaged quite severely, but fortunately most of the tooling was still in a usable condition and could be put back to work. Here, Hirst was able to set in motion the production of a new series of saloon models. These were based upon the chassis of the two-wheel-drive Kübelwagen (Type 82) and were effectively what had been known under German control as the Type 82E, except that they were fitted with the

larger 1131cc, 25bhp engine. These vehicles were later redesignated the Type 51 by Hirst, the Type 53 being a sunroof model while the Type 55 was to have been a cabriolet. The Type 82 Kübel was retitled the Type 21 but, of course, never saw production again.

It was impossible for the factory to remain under British military control for any longer than was absolutely necessary, but the matter of who should run it first needed to be resolved. Hirst set about appointing a new management structure, with its members being taken from those VW personnel who had successfully come through the de-Nazification process that was taking place in Germany, along with a few "outsiders". The whole process was a mass of confusion, according to Ivan Hirst, as he recalled that some members of the new management were considered unacceptable by his superiors and had to be replaced, only to be reinstated following an appeal.

Eventually, after what Hirst referred to as a game of musical chairs, a relatively stable management was established and the task of undertaking full-scale production was ready to be addressed. As far as production workers were concerned, most were recruited from PoWs currently being released from holding camps in the British Zone, while others were local townspeople who had worked at the factory in the past.

British Control

Holding the whole structure together was a British board which was also responsible for the newly named town of Wolfsburg, with Major Hirst and an assistant looking after financial matters and Colonel Charles Radclyffe taking responsibility for the industrial side. Ivan Hirst, although always heralded as being the man responsible for getting the Volkswagen back on its feet, always keenly emphasized that it was a team effort, with Germans and British working alongside each other towards a common goal.

When Germany surrendered at the end of World War II, the matter of wartime reparations was raised – a system whereby other countries could claim some form of damages against Germany for the losses and costs incurred fighting the Nazis. A list of possible assets was drawn up, with Wolfsburg not unnaturally being included. One of the first to show an interest was Australia, a country that had never had a worthwhile engineering industry of its own. However, because the factory was being used for the repair of military vehicles, the MilGov had placed a four-year reserve on Wolfsburg, and Australia was not prepared to wait that long.

Another possible new owner was America, with the Ford factory showing a good deal of interest in the plant. The MilGov organization was quite taken with the idea of Ford having control, as it was felt that there were many advantages to a car manufacturing company running the Volkswagen factory. Ford, of course, already had a plant at Cologne. Hirst attended a number of meetings, which included representatives from Ford in Great Britain, only to discover that they, too, shared many of the problems which beset the Volkswagen factory, the worst being a shortage of raw materials. Hirst so impressed the people from Ford that he was offered a job, but politely turned it down, preferring to see the Volkswagen project through to completion. Some time later, in 1948, Henry Ford II visited the Wolfsburg plant for talks with Charles Radclyffe, but when he realized how close the site was to the Soviet Zone, he lost interest. Anti-Communist feelings ran high in the USA at the time.

Another possible new keeper was the British Rootes organization under the leadership of Sir William, later Lord, Rootes. He made a trip to Wolfsburg to take a look at the machine tools which were in use there, most notably a large press used to stamp out the roof sections. However, this particular piece of equipment had been damaged beyond economic repair in the war, so Rootes began to lose interest. Ivan Hirst showed him round the remainder of the factory and told the British industrialist of his plan to put the Volkswagen back into production. Sir William politely smiled and said to Hirst, "It's been a nice day, young man, but if you think you're going to get any cars built here, you're a fool!". Many years later, Lord Rootes confessed to Wing Commander Berryman, also of the MilGov organization, that he should perhaps have shown rather more interest.

Close Inspection

With the war against Japan still under way, arrangements were made later in 1945 for a number of engineering specialists to visit Germany to examine first-hand the latest techniques employed by German industry. According to Ivan Hirst, the principal objective of this tour was to see if anything could be learnt that might be put to use in the war in the Far East. However, although Japan surrendered not long after hostilities came to an end in Europe, two Volkswagens were still transported back to the United Kingdom for further investigation at the Humber factory. There, technicians examined the cars in detail and came to the somewhat surprising decision that there was little they could learn from the Volkswagen design. Considering how crude the majority of British vehicles were at the time, this view was clearly short-sighted.

It was around this time, in 1946, that an interesting variation on the Beetle was built at the factory. Colonel Michael McEvoy, his interest in motorsport not having been dulled by almost six long years of war, came to Hirst one day and suggested they build a Volkswagen-based racing car.

Hirst was less than impressed with the idea, rightly believing that the factory had more than enough on its plate without getting side-tracked with such a whimsical project. However, McEvoy's enthusiasm did set Hirst thinking, so he sketched out an idea for a two-seat Volkswagen roadster and asked Rudolph Ringel, head of the experimental shop, to build a prototype. This car was offered by Hirst to Colonel Charles Radclyffe, his chief at headquarters, for use during the summer months. Subsequently known by enthusiasts the world over as "the Radclyffe Roadster", the attractive two-seater saw regular use before eventually disappearing, probably scrapped by Volkswagen personnel. The same fate almost certainly befell a crude cabriolet Beetle which Hirst had Ringel build for his personal use.

At this time, two well-established coachbuilding companies approached Volkswagen with regard to producing convertible Beetles. One of these was Wilhelm Karmann GmbH, the other Joseph Hebmüller and Sons. Karmann, of Osnabrück, had a long history of building high-quality cabriolets based on a variety of chassis from companies such as Hansa-Lloyd and Adler. After the war, Karmann visited Wolfsburg with a view to buying a Volkswagen chassis on which to build a convertible Beetle. However, due to the restrictions placed on German citizens which prevented them from buying a car at this time, Karmann was unsuccessful in his approach. However, his persistence paid off and, in November 1946, he was given the 10,000th car to be built since the war.

Further chassis were soon made available and two prototypes were built at the Karmann works. The first of these was a crude conversion with external hinges on the hood mechanism and no rear window. The second was much improved, with wind-down rear-side windows, a glass rear window and a more sophisticated hood frame. However, with no fixed roof, excessive chassis flex was a major problem, necessitating the addition of a substantial reinforcing member under each sill. Despite the success of the Karmann prototypes, all talk of series production was fruitless due to a lack of the essential raw materials, such as sheet steel and fabric for the folding roof. Not for a further two years was Karmann able to resume work in earnest.

Expanding Horizons

Hebmüller's story was similar to that of Karmann, with official permission being granted to build a series of prototypes which, with Volkswagen's approval, would make way for a production run. Once the problems of a lack of rigidity had been overcome, Hebmüller was able to satisfy Volkswagen that his roadster was ready for production. However, there were political moves afoot in Germany which would have a profound effect on the future of the company.

Hirst and Radclyffe were confident that the Beetle had a future and, in 1947, visited the Paris Motor Show to take a look at the opposition, so to speak. Few cars impressed them other than the Skoda, which was also a rear-engined, small car, although water- rather than air-cooled. On their return to Wolfsburg, the matter of who would take over the running of the factory was raised again. Times were changing in Europe, with the Soviet Union, formerly an ally, becoming more and more isolationist in its outlook. It would possibly soon not be wise for the British to have a presence so close to the Soviet sector in Germany.

In the meantime, Ben Pon arrived at Wolfsburg wishing to order some cars. He was the strong-willed Dutchman to whom Ferdinand Porsche had agreed to make available the first export models once the war was over. Considering the vehement anti-German feelings held by the majority of the Dutch, Pon was clearly either foolish or a man convinced of the Beetle's worth. How else could someone expect to sell a German product in post-war Holland? However, history was to prove that Pon was certainly no fool. His order for six cars was duly accepted, but when he returned to the factory to collect them, only five were ready, the sixth having fallen foul of the somewhat unreliable production line. This episode nonetheless marked the fulfilment of the first export order for a Volkswagen.

Hirst began the search for a person qualified to head the factory, and started to interview suitable people. He came to hear of one Heinz Nordhoff, formerly of Opel. There, he had been responsible for overseeing Opel truck production and, as a result, had been awarded an honorary title of Economic Leader during the war. This title prevented him from holding any executive position at a German facility in the US sector – the Americans considered him possibly to have too many Nazi connections, although this proved not to be the case. As the British were less stringent in such matters, Hirst asked to see Nordhoff, with a view to his becoming a second in command at Wolfsburg. However, following two days of intensive interviewing, the former Opel man made such an impression on Hirst that he recommended him to the MilGov organization as a suitable head of the factory. Nordhoff was interviewed by Charles Radclyffe and then, as of 1 January 1948, he was appointed General Director of Volkswagen.

By the end of 1947, vehicle production had reached some 2,500 per month, although the previous winter prospects had looked bleak when a shortage of coal meant that the whole plant had to be shut down due to a lack of power. Only by striking a deal with the nearby town of Braunschweig, whereby coal was swapped for electricity, could the power station be reopened. Other deals were also struck: a shortage of

carburettor parts lead Hirst to visit the nearby Voigtlander camera plant to persuade them to make carburettor floats and jets. It was not unknown for completed Volkswagens, destined for the army, to mysteriously disappear in exchange for sheet metal or other materials.

As time progressed, supplies became more readily available and the demand for cars increased at a rate that surprised even Hirst. When German currency reform took place, in June 1948, the economy expanded at a great rate. Suddenly the German people became more wealthy and the prospect of owning their own cars became more achievable. By the end of the year, Wolfsburg was removed from the reparations list and allowed to breathe a little more easily. The British began to withdraw from the factory, allowing the German management to take greater responsibility. Hirst himself was demobilized during the winter of 1947/48 but remained at Wolfsburg, in a largely civilian role, to work alongside Nordhoff for what he describes as a fairly uncomfortable year and a half. He plainly felt that, if Nordhoff was to succeed, he should be allowed to run things for himself, in his own way. The MilGov board agreed and Hirst left Wolfsburg in the control of the man from Opel. Late in 1949, Charles Radclyffe finally handed the factory over to the German Minister of Economics, bringing to a close a remarkable period in the company's history.

Right Despite shortages of raw materials, production at Wolfsburg gradually continued to increase. The 1,000th car built in March 1946 was cause for celebration as, less than a year earlier, the future had looked very bleak.

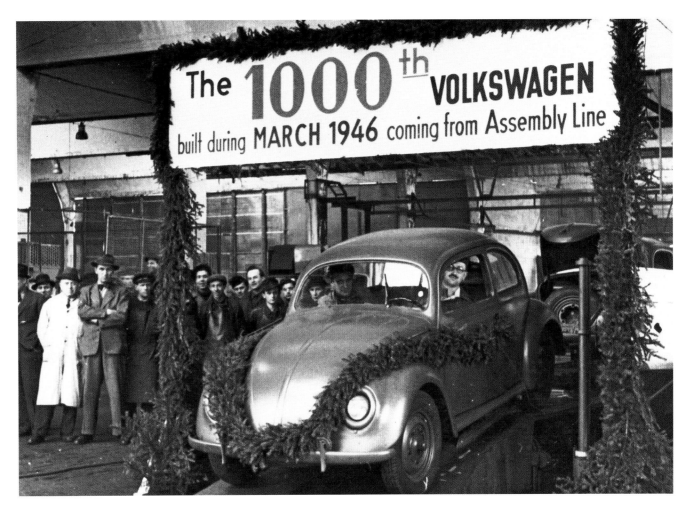

The 1000th VOLKSWAGEN built during MARCH 1946 coming from Assembly Line

One of the first decisions made by Nordhoff was to give the go-ahead to Karmann and Hebmüller to commence production of their cabriolets, which they manufactured from vehicles delivered to them by VW. The two companies eventually began work in earnest, Hebmüller's first production model leaving the works in Wulfrath in June 1949, and Karmann's in Osnabrück in September. Everything looked fine for the two companies until, just one month into production, Hebmüller's workshops caught fire and were all but destroyed. Quite how the fire started remains a mystery but, following a great effort, work resumed just four weeks later. Unfortunately, Hebmüller never really recovered from this disaster and the company went into decline in 1950, eventually ceasing operations in 1951. Production of the Hebmüller roadster was transferred to the Karmann works at Osnabrück, where a further 14 examples were built, bringing the total to just 696.

Karmann fared better throughout this period, with cabriolet production growing steadily until the model became a profitable sideline to the saloon. Indeed, as time would eventually prove, the cabriolet was destined to become the last remaining Beetle variant to be built in Germany.

But what of Ferdinand Porsche all this time? Sadly, the far-sighted Doctor was never to play a part in seeing his beloved People's Car reach production, for he was imprisoned by the French, subjected to post-war internment after having been accused of employing forced labour by Pierre Peugeot, head of the French car company of the same name. The real motive behind Peugeot's incriminating outburst was probably the fact that Porsche had been invited to France by Marcel Paul, the French Minister for Industrial Production, with a view to designing a "French Volkswagen", a vehicle which would almost certainly have had a dramatic effect on the finances of existing French companies. Porsche's designs did eventually surface, somewhat modified, in the form of the Renault 4CV.

Porsche was held in prison, often in very poor conditions considering his age, until 1947. He was finally released when witnesses came forward to prove that, far from employing forced French labour, Porsche had in fact done whatever he could to prevent French citizens from being forcibly moved to Germany to work in his factory. His period of imprisonment did little to help the ageing Doctor who, by this time, was over 70 years old. He suffered prolonged ill-health and died on 30 January 1951, never fully to witness the amazing success story of his dream car. •

far horizons

The new decade began with Volkswagen at last looking like it had a future. For almost five years since the end of World War II, the factory had endured hardships almost beyond comprehension, ranging from shortages of raw materials, labour and power, to political pushing and shoving as various governments expressed their interest – or lack of it – in the company. Only when the British finally took a firm hold of Volkswagen and then appointed Heinz Nordhoff as General Director, did the future begin to look more rosy.

By January 1950, some 86,182 Beetles had been built, although that name had not yet found its way into popular parlance. In fact, nobody can really be sure where that name came from: Ferdinand Porsche is credited with having referred to his car before the war as having the shape of a May beetle, while the American press is said to have called the car a "beetle" in the late 1940s. In Britain, the original importer, John Colborne-Baber, drove a VW and the pair were referred to as "Colborne-Baber and his funny little beetle". All that's important is that the name stuck.

The first major milestone had been achieved in 1946 when, on 14 October, the 10,000th Beetle rolled off the assembly line. However, only a further 20 cars were to be built that year. Production sky-rocketed, in relative terms, in 1950 under Nordhoff's leadership when a total of 81,979 Beetles were assembled, almost double the production figure for the previous year. Many thought that Nordhoff had been crazy to increase production but he was right to make the decision for, at one point, there had been a waiting list of some 15,000 customers in Germany alone, along with a further 7,000 in other countries. Only by doubling production could Nordhoff guarantee being able to satisfy the demand and he was well aware that, although Volkswagen may have had a head start over most other German car manufacturers immediately after the war, it was only a matter of time before his competitors would re-establish themselves and be able to compete on equal terms with his company.

The problem for Nordhoff was that the company did not have the money to be able to expand in the way he wished. While the currency reform of 1948 (which replaced the Reichsmark with a new Deutschmark) gave the man in the street a new-found wealth because the currency was stabilized, it effectively reduced Volkswagen's bank balance to zero as, up until then, all financial dealings had been based on the old Reichsmark, which was now worthless on the world market. Realizing that he was caught in the classic Catch 22 situation (no money meant no cars – no cars meant no money), Nordhoff contacted each of his dealers in Germany and asked them to bring to the factory as many of the new Deutschmarks as they could muster. It is a measure of the respect in which Nordhoff was held that the dealers responded by arriving at Wolfsburg with suitcases filled with money. It seems that most, if not all, realized that if they were to have a future they would have to be prepared to invest in the product.

The New World

Nordhoff was undoubtedly a man of vision, for he seemed able to see far into the future at a time when most people were still talking about the past. He knew that to survive Volkswagen needed to expand its horizons far beyond the borders of Germany and Europe – America was the key to the company's long-term success, he felt. He also appreciated, as did Ivan Hirst before him, that it would be important to ensure that there was an adequate supply of spare parts so that cars could be satisfactorily serviced.

The first car which Nordhoff attempted to sell into the USA arrived there on 17 January 1949, and marked the beginning of the American love affair with the VW. The Beetle arrived on board the *Westerdam*, accompanied by Ben Pon, the enthusiastic Dutchman who had succeeded in persuading his own fellow countrymen to buy Volkswagens, even when anti-German feeling in his homeland was at its height. Pon had been sent as an envoy to the USA by Nordhoff, and his brief was to assess the potential for selling the humble Volkswagen to a car-crazy America.

Right   Stock lined up ready for despatch from Wolfsburg in 1956.

To set the ball rolling, an American colleague of Pon's arranged to hold a press conference on board the merchant vessel carrying that first "American" Volkswagen. Unfortunately for Pon and Nordhoff, the car received a lot of bad publicity. Despite constantly referring to the VW as the "Victory Wagen" in an effort to hide its origins, Pon was unable to persuade the Americans that the Beetle was anything other than Hitler's People's Car.

Once the car was off-loaded, Pon felt he would be able to overcome the scepticism, but he remained unable to convince the American public of its potential. He approached several automobile showrooms in an effort to enlist them as official Volkswagen agents, but again met with a lack of interest. He soon ran low on funds and was eventually forced to sell the "sample" Volkswagen, and some spares he had brought with him, for $800 to a Swedish dealer by the name of Vaughn, in order to pay his hotel bill and fund his return fare.

Pon wrote to Nordhoff, saying, "It is too early to try to sell Volkswagens in the United States. Dealers selling European cars there don't know how to service them". It seems that other importers had messed up the market for Volkswagen by convincing the public that all imports were unreliable and expensive to maintain. The news

saddened Nordhoff, for Volkswagen desperately needed some dollars with which to buy machinery and tooling from the USA. At the time, few countries were interested in receiving payment in the form of Deutschmarks. Nordhoff made the decision to visit the United States himself to see if he could solve the problem but he, too, met with the same reluctance that Pon had encountered. Nobody, it seems, believed the Volkswagen Beetle had a future, especially in the USA. The American motoring press was very critical of the product, feeling that it had nothing to offer that could not be provided by Detroit on a grander scale.

But a little over a year after Ben Pon's unsuccessful visit, Nordhoff made a fresh attempt to win over the American market by appointing an exclusive US agent, a foreign car distributor by the name of Maximilian

Hoffman from Chicago. Made responsible for all territories to the east of the Mississippi, Hoffman succeeded in selling no fewer than 330 Volkswagens in 1950 but, while at first sight that may have seemed impressive, the American public bought a total of over 6.6 million other cars in that year.

Early US Sales

Hoffman was a born salesman and adopted aggressive sales tactics. If he was approached by trade customers who wished to buy his more exotic Jaguars and other sports cars from him, Hoffman would occasionally suggest they stood a better chance of getting a favourable deal if they bought a Volkswagen or two. His strong-arm tactics worked well and many dealers soon discovered they could sell the Volkswagen more easily than their range of sports cars. On one occasion, a dealer arrived at Hoffman's and was asked if he had come to collect his usual quota of sports cars but instead replied that no, he had come to collect a few more VWs – they were proving to be rather good sellers.

Those early American sales, however, were erratic and, even though there was an increasing number of dealers handling Volkswagen's affairs in North America, Nordhoff was acutely aware there had been no effective sales strategy. What he wanted was a properly co-ordinated sales team working throughout the continent. However, Max Hoffman had always been a foreign car importer first and foremost and selling Volkswagens was only a small, albeit profitable, part of his business. He was not really too interested in the customer, but concerned himself more with selling vehicles to other dealers who could then also be responsible for servicing and supplying spare parts.

This situation was in conflict with Nordhoff's (and Hirst's) ideals, whereby cars should only be sold where there is an adequate after-sales operation to look after them. He realized it would be necessary for Volkswagen to establish a full network of dealers across the country, with a full service operation to keep the cars on the road. There was no point in trying to persuade someone to buy a strange foreign car if the owner could not get it fixed when it went wrong, Nordhoff kept telling his people. What was happening in the USA was, therefore, in total conflict with his belief that you must have a sales team backed up by an efficient service network, as was the case throughout Europe and the rest of the world. There, people were buying Volkswagen products, not only because they felt they were good vehicles, but also because they had confidence in the service and spares programme.

The agreement which existed between Max Hoffman and Volkswagen finally came to an end in 1953. This left America wide open as far as VW sales were concerned, so Nordhoff, painfully aware of the fact that neither he nor his managers at Wolfsburg had any idea of how to tackle the market, studied a map of North America and divided the country into two halves – one to the east and the other to the west of the Mississippi river. On the western side, where the Beetle had already gained considerable respect, VW's sales representative was Geoffrey Lange. Lange found to Nordhoff's pleasure that a lot of good work had been done by a customer of Max Hoffman, John von Neumann of California, who had appreciated the finer points of the Porsche-designed Volkswagen from the very beginning. Lange, much to Nordhoff's relief, was soon able to bring some order to the confusion which had previously reigned in the USA.

A Sixth Sense

To cover the areas to the east of the Mississippi dividing line, Nordhoff sent Will Van de Kamp across to the USA. Van de Kamp had previously

LIMOUSINE

STANDARD- UND EXPORT-MODELL

worked as a field representative for Volkswagen in Germany and was someone with unshakable confidence in the products Wolfsburg had to offer. He was soon able to persuade potential dealers of the benefits of becoming part of the Volkswagen sales network. Van de Kamp arrived in the USA in January 1954 and from the word go appeared to have the powers of a clairvoyant when it came to choosing new Volkswagen dealers. While others might have taken the more obvious route of appointing established automotive retailers, Van de Kamp often chose to give someone an agency because he had a type of "sixth sense" about that person's abilities. With Geoffrey Lange in the west and Van de Kamp in the east, Nordhoff was pleased to be able to establish a network of dealers across America which would still be recognizable almost a quarter of a century later.

Quite why the American public suddenly appeared to take a shine to the Volkswagen cannot be entirely explained by Lange's or Van de Kamp's enthusiasm. After all, no matter how good the salesman is, you still have to tempt the customer into the showroom. It is possible that, by the early 1950s, the American public was becoming used to the thought of buying imported products of all types. Motoring enthusiasts in the USA had long appreciated that if you wanted a fine-handling sports car

you had to look towards Europe. On the west coast of America, and in Hollywood in particular, cars such as British Jaguars and Italian Ferraris were becoming very popular with celebrities of the period. The family man might not be able to afford such exotic machines, but the high-profile display of imported cars among the film star fraternity must have helped break down resistance to buying a foreign car.

VWoA Is Born

Unfortunately, Will Van de Kamp's runaway enthusiasm for the Beetle and the sales network was his undoing. In Nordhoff's eyes, Van de Kamp made the mistake of considering the American market as belonging to him, rather than to Volkswagen. As the eastern dealer network became more efficient, there was less call for a trouble-shooter, or for someone to set up new outlets. Van de Kamp's success was ultimately his downfall when, in April 1955, Volkswagen of America was set up to take direct control of the US market, and Carl Hahn was appointed Van de Kamp's successor. However, his undeniable talents did not go to waste as he continued to be involved with one of the many VW agencies he had helped to get started.

Hahn's instruction from Wolfsburg's General Director was to appoint further dealerships but, this time, to concentrate on enlisting the

support of those who wished to have sole agencies, i.e., dealerships which only offered Volkswagens for sale – previously, most Volkswagen dealers also sold what might have been considered rival products. Nordhoff had other ideas up his sleeve, too. He felt that Carl Hahn should target people who previously did not even sell cars of any sort, let alone rivals, suggesting that the best existing operations had probably already been picked by American manufacturers.

Hahn placed an even greater emphasis on service back-up than had Van de Kamp, capitalizing on the fact that many other imported cars, and especially those from Great Britain, let their customers down in this vital area. One of the first changes that Hahn and Volkswagen's export chief, Manuel Hinke, carried out was to redesign the American sales network and, in its place, to set up a single sales operation which would gradually lessen the importance placed on the west coast. Thanks to the determination of Nordhoff, Hahn and Hinke to conquer the US market, Volkswagen of America went from strength to strength, impressing customers with its excellent sales and service network.

Success Story

A measure of its success throughout the 1950s can be seen from studying a table of US registrations between 1949, when Ben Pon made his

appearance aboard the *Westerdam*, and 1960. Export efforts were very much concentrated on the USA in order to raise much-needed dollars.

1949–1960 USA registrations

Year	VWs registered
1949	2
1950	157
1951	390
1952	611
1953	1,013
1954	6,614
1955	30,928
1956	55,690
1957	79,524
1958	104,306
1959	150,601
1960	191,372

It is interesting to compare these figures with German sales and total worldwide production over a similar period.

1950–1959 German registrations

Year	German sales	(worldwide production)
1950	50,562	(81,779)
1951	58,469	(93,709)
1952	71,440	(114,348)
1953	80,157	(151,323)
1954	113,169	(202,174)
1955	128,687	(279,986)
1956	141,979	(333,190)
1957	160,781	(380,561)
1958	186,014	(451,526)
1959	228,234	(575,407)

However, none of the foregoing quite explains why the Volkswagen

Beetle (or "Bug" as it had affectionately become known in the USA) should have become such a successful product on the American market. After all, with cheap and plentiful fuel, a freeway network that was the envy of the world and relatively traffic-free roads, it could be argued that there was no need for a small, fuel-efficient car. Already by the mid-1950s, though, there was a growing body of technically-aware people for whom the regular American cars with their huge fins and vast expanses of chrome were of little interest. Some people simply appreciated the finer points of the Volkswagen's engineering, while others regarded the Volkswagen as a basic form of transport that allowed them to stand out from the crowd. For many, the fascination with the VW was a result of a thrifty, "waste not, want not" outlook, or in many cases it was simply because a parent owned a Beetle which was handed down from father – or more frequently, mother – to son or daughter.

There are many stories of how people were won over to the VW way of life, such as that told by Gene Berg, one of the founding fathers of the Volkswagen performance industry in the USA. His introduction to the Volkswagen was due to an uncle who owned a 1955 model. At the time, Gene was typical of many carefree Americans, driving a 1940 Ford coupé with a tuned flathead V8 engine. However, the fact that his uncle's little Volkswagen could drive

along muddy tracks in conditions so bad that a person could hardly stand, let alone walk, made a huge impression. When Gene got married a year or two later and needed economical transport, he ordered himself a Beetle. He always clearly remembered the cost of that new, black Volkswagen sedan: $1,680, or roughly a dollar per pound in weight.

Many other Americans had developed a familiarity with the Volkswagen while serving with the army in Germany, either during or immediately after World War II. In the months following the end of hostilities, the only means of transport available to the GIs, other than the worn-out military vehicles, were Volkswagens that had been abandoned by the retreating German Army. More often than not, these were Type 82 Kübelwagens which, of course, used essentially the same engine and running gear as the early Beetles. When the German economy eventually recovered following the currency reform, Volkswagens were virtually the only form of private transportation available. It is, therefore, unsurprising that many American soldiers would have become familiar with the sight of the VW, while many of them would have owned one during their service there.

Although Volkswagen did not officially export Beetles to America

until the early 1950s, a number of cars are known to have found their way "home" courtesy of soldiers returning to the USA – they made practical souvenirs of their owner's time spent in Europe! Almost everyone who came into contact with the VW under those circumstances came away impressed with the way it could cope with even the most ham-fisted attempts by military personnel to maintain the cars with the minimum of loving care, or to drive them into the ground, safe

in the knowledge that a replacement would not be far away. In many ways, the situation was reminiscent of the pre-war test programme, during which the VW30 prototypes had been driven mercilessly by members of the German military in an attempt to find the vehicle's weak points.

Classic Advertising

Tales of the car's indestructibility and character grew by the day. Hundreds

Right The brochure for the Type 2 was keen to show just some of its many guises.

of jokes were circulated about the Beetle – how they are so unreliable you have to carry a spare motor in the trunk, for example (America wasn't used to rear engines!) – but they all helped to enhance the car's mystique. The master stroke was when, in 1959, the Doyle, Dane, Bernbach advertising agency was given the contract to promote Volkswagen in America. Once the campaign got under way, there seemed to be no looking back, for instead of ignoring or being wary of the jokes, Doyle, Dane, Bernbach turned them to VW's advantage. DDB made no attempt to pretty the car up, by making it look more glamorous or implying it was bigger than it really was. In contrast, most rival car advertising at the time (and since) consistently made claims that were hard to swallow.

While many others used air-brushed illustrations to display their vehicles, Volkswagen's agency chose to use real photographs, frequently of older, used models to impress on the customer that the Beetle was not just another part of America's throw-away society. "What you see is what you get" could have been the VW motto. The Doyle, Dane, Bernbach campaign rapidly became part of Volkswagen folklore, with many of the press advertisements becoming an art-form all of their own. Several have become classics, such as the famous "Lemon" ad of 1960, which spoke of Volkswagen's stringent quality control system, or

the later "Think Small" campaign which told of the economical nature of the VW. Every DDB advert helped to create an image of reliability, individuality and value for money that set Volkswagen's Beetle apart from the Detroit mainstream.

The specification and design of the Beetle changed quite noticeably throughout the 1950s, although it never lost its basic character. By 1950, the Beetle had become only slightly more sophisticated than the first KdF-Wagens that had appeared a little over ten years earlier. At the front of the car, Porsche's torsion-bar suspension was still in use, consisting of two sets of multi-leaf torsion bars housed in a pair of transverse axle tubes. Drum brakes were still used, operated by a system of rods and cables. At the rear, a pair of torsion bars were connected to trailing arms which, in turn, located on the outer end of the swing-axle drive shafts. Cable-operated drum brakes were to be found here also. The front shock absorbers were conventional telescopic hydraulic units, but those at the rear were of the older-style lever-arm design.

The chassis itself closely resembled the flat floorpan favoured by Porsche, although more strengthening ribs were used, further to increase rigidity. Rear-seat passengers would have approved of the improvement in leg room, brought about by lowering the floorpan behind the front seats.

Mechanically, the new decade

began with the Beetle making use of the 1131cc, 25bhp unit, first introduced in the Type 82 Kübelwagen back in 1943. The engine had proved itself to be extremely reliable, if not over-powerful, and Nordhoff saw no reason why the unit should be changed. He felt that efforts should be directed towards making the car a better product in terms of finish and overall specification. Similarly, the transmission was very much like that used in previous years, although the casing was now ribbed for greater strength, unlike the smoother design seen on the KdF-Wagen.

Constant Change

In July 1949, Volkswagen had introduced an "export" version of the Beetle, which was designed to appeal to foreign markets where there was greater competition from rival products. These export-specification cars came with chromed hubcaps, door handles, headlamp rims and bumpers, polished aluminium body trim and a new two-spoke ivory-coloured steering wheel which replaced the black, three-spoke design of the standard model. While the standard model came in semi-gloss grey paint, the export VW could be had in a range of high-gloss colours including green, blue, red, beige and black. Inside the export model, the interior trim was of a higher quality while the dashboard now featured a removable

panel to the right of the speedometer to allow a clock to be fitted.

One problem that had come to light, particularly in cold climates, was the lack of adequate ventilation in the Beetle. With the windows rolled up, the car soon became stuffy, a situation made worse when the heater was used. Volkswagen overcame this problem, to a degree, in 1950 when it added small cut-outs to the leading edge of the door glass, allowing fresh, draught-free air into the car simply by winding the window down very slightly. The following year, small opening vents were added to the front quarter-panels ahead of the doors which ducted air into the car from below the dashboard. However, this system lasted for less than two years as it proved to be very draughty, earning the vents the nickname of "crotch coolers" in the USA as the fresh air was directed where the occupants least appreciated it!

In the early 1950s, two significant improvements to the car were the change to hydraulic brakes on all export models in 1950 and the adoption of telescopic rear shock absorbers in 1951. Between them, these two improvements made what was already becoming a good car even better. The standard model was forced to soldier on with the dreadfully antiquated cable-brake system, however, and owners had to prepare themselves for the brakes to lock on in very cold weather as the cables became frozen in their guides.

Out With The Old

The next, and arguably the most noticeable, stage in the Beetle's development took place in 1953 when the split rear window, which had been part of the Beetle's design since the KdF prototypes, made way for a single oval-shaped window which offered some 23 per cent greater area. With this, and a dashboard that had been radically redesigned the previous year, the Beetle took on a considerably more modern appearance. The only drawback to this redesign (at least, as far as future collectors and restorers were concerned) was that a small industry sprang up with several workshops offering to cut the central dividing bar out of the old split-window cars to mimic the new look! Export models also benefited from synchromesh being incorporated on the top three gears in the transmission, making the Beetle far more pleasant to drive. As far as the factory was concerned, the greatest news was that the 500,000th Beetle finally rolled off the assembly line on 3 July 1953. The Volkswagen was clearly here to stay.

The trusty 1131cc, 25bhp engine, which had provided the motivation behind the Kübelwagen, Schwimmwagen and the first production Beetles, was finally redesigned for 1954 and grew to 1192cc and 30bhp. This engine, although of essentially the same layout as its predecessor, allowed the Beetle to cruise at between 8 and 16km/h (5 and 10mph) faster, and proved to be one of the most reliable engines ever built by Volkswagen. As a measure of its success, the same engine remained in production until the end of the decade, seeing service in all Volkswagen models. Even as late as the 1960s, the engine was available in the standard sedan and was still popular for such applications as fire-pumps and generators.

On 5 August 1955, the 1,000,000th Beetle was produced at Wolfsburg, a milestone which Heinz Nordhoff celebrated by announcing a cut in the purchase price. The Standard model was cut from DM3,950 to DM3,790, the Export from DM4,850 to DM4,700 and the cabriolet from DM6,500 to DM5,990. Throughout the year, several improvements were made to the car, including the fitting of flashing indicators for the American market in place of the traditional semaphores. Surprisingly, the cars produced for other markets, including Germany, retained the out-dated mechanical indicators which, as always, were mounted in the door "B" pillar. US-specification models also gained the unwieldy "towel rail" bumper guards which were designed to bring the VW's bumper height up to something closer to that of the average domestic US car. Both of these modifications were introduced in August 1955 in readiness for cars that were to be released in the 1956 model year.

The Beetle then remained virtually unchanged until August 1957 when the rear window was enlarged by a massive 95 per cent, while the windscreen grew by 17 per cent. The result was a car which felt altogether less claustrophobic than previous years' models. At the rear, the appearance of the engine lid was substantially changed for the first time since the KdF-Wagen appeared. The familiar "W" design with its strongly defined swage lines gave way to a smoother, simpler engine lid which was to see service virtually unchanged for another ten years. Inside the car, the dashboard was totally redesigned, too, with a larger glove box, provisions for a radio in the centre of the panel and grilles either side of the speedometer, one of which could house an optional loudspeaker.

The Beetle remained in essentially this form for the remainder of the decade, but it is worth noting that it was no longer the only product being offered by Volkswagen in the 1950s. In the first year of the new decade, Volkswagen announced a new model known as the Type 2. This was a Beetle-inspired commercial vehicle based on a sketch made by the indefatigable Ben Pon during a visit to the factory. Pon correctly surmised that there was a need for a reliable commercial vehicle which could be driven and easily maintained by the small businessman. As the German economy was slowly recovering from the ravages of war, many small companies sprang up to capitalize on the new-found wealth. These businesses needed a vehicle which offered the reliability of a Volkswagen yet could cope with carrying a useful payload.

New Arrivals

Pon's sketch consisted of a box-like body mounted on what was more or less a Beetle chassis. While this particular layout proved to be impractical – the Beetle floorpan was not strong enough to carry a large load placed in the centre – the idea appealed to Nordhoff who gave the go-ahead to design and produce a suitable vehicle. The end result was a simple, one-piece body welded onto a chassis frame which was far stronger than the saloon's floorpan. The trusty 1131cc, 25bhp engine was pressed into service, as was the Beetle's transmission – with one notable modification. In order to increase the ground clearance, reduction boxes were fitted to either end of the rear axle shafts in exactly the same way as on the old Type 82 Kübelwagen. At the front, a new, heavy-duty suspension unit was used, based on the design used on passenger cars.

The Type 2, or "Bulli" as it became affectionately known, proved to be a huge success, seeing regular use with all kinds of businesses and even the emergency services. One of the most popular conversions was into the role of ambulance –

the factory even offered such a conversion themselves. In later years, the Type 2 would become the mainstay of the motor caravan or "camper" market, earning itself an unparalleled reputation for longevity and reliability the world over.

The second new product to appear in the 1950s was the stylish Karmann Ghia, in both coupé and cabriolet form. Following the success of the Karmann-built Beetle cabriolets, consideration was given to producing a somewhat more glamorous model designed to appeal to a wider audience. Wilhelm Karmann had long held a desire to build a sports car of his own and talks took place between the Osnabrück works and Wolfsburg, with a view to producing a Volkswagen-based sports car. Heinz Nordhoff was not particularly interested in the idea as all his thoughts – and the factory's spare capacity – were being taken up with producing the Beetle in sufficient quantities to meet the ever-increasing demand.

Others might have given up at this first hurdle, but Karmann persisted, eventually persuading Nordhoff to allow him to submit some designs. These were duly examined by Ludwig Boehner, head of production development, and Karl Feuereissen, head of the sales and service operation. Both were impressed with the overall concept but remained unmoved by the styling. So Karmann turned to the well-established Ghia styling studio in Turin for inspiration

and the result was a beautiful, timeless two-seat coupé, the design credits for which have always been hotly contested by both parties.

The Karmann Ghia, as the new car came to be called, was eventually given Nordhoff's blessing and went into production in 1955, to be met with universal praise. In America, the Karmann Ghia became extremely popular, being criticized only for its rather lacklustre performance. After

all, despite their svelte good looks, the stylish coupé and its cabriolet stable mate relied only on an unmodified Volkswagen drivetrain.

With the Beetle going from strength to strength, increasing export sales, a successful commercial vehicle and a sports car of its own, Volkswagen could look forward to the next decade with a confidence few other automobile manufacturers could match. •

Above   The 1958 Karmann Ghia looked stunning in this 1958 brochure; little wonder that the car was a hit.

time for change

If the 1950s saw the Volkswagen Beetle become well and truly established on the world market, then the 1960s would see it undergo several major revisions that were intended to keep it there. The new decade began modestly enough, with Volkswagen making few changes to the car other than detail modifications to the interior – for example, a new steering wheel with semi-circular horn ring for the 1960 models at last replaced the rather dated one that had been in place since the mid-fifties – or adding an anti-roll bar for the front suspension. Probably the most useful change as far as the driver was concerned was the self-cancelling indicator arm.

Lower Saxony believed Volkswagen to belong to its people, while the German government felt it was a national asset. Finally, the problems were resolved when the company was floated on the stock exchange on 22 August 1960. However, the government in Bonn retained a 20 per cent stake, with another 20 per cent held by Lower Saxony – the remaining 60 per cent was offered to the public to raise further capital.

As a result of this course of action, the Volkswagen purse swelled from DM300 million in 1959 to around DM600 million in 1960, providing the factory with the wherewithal to invest in new projects. With 3.6 million shares on offer, there was no shortage of investors at the initial price of DM50 per share. Just over one year later, Volkswagen announced that the shares had increased in value by around 12 per cent, providing a healthy return for those investors who wished to make a quick financial killing.

The other big news, so far as the factory was concerned, was the increase in productivity, with Heinz Nordhoff proudly being able to announce that daily Beetle production had topped the 4,000 mark.

However, no matter how many cars Wolfsburg was able to produce, it was still unable to keep up with demand. In 1960, Volkswagen dealers were still having to quote a five-month delivery time for the car, in stark contrast to rivals who could guarantee delivery within a few weeks at the most. Perhaps it was time for Volkswagen to make some big decisions if it was to keep hold of its number one spot in the market place. Nordhoff, for all his leadership qualities, did at times appear to remain complacent about the company's products, giving the impression that the Beetle was all that Volkswagen needed to stay at the top. However, as time would unquestionably prove, appearances can be deceiving.

As a whole, the German motor industry was expanding, with total vehicle production exceeding 2,000,000 units in 1960. As far as Volkswagen was concerned, production reached 725,939 cars – just over 700,000 of which were export models – and some 139,919

Type 2 commercials. The factory's fortunes continued to improve, with a turnover of some DM4.6 billion for 1960. In Germany there were now over 1,300 VW dealers, with a further 4,000 to be found overseas. Together they helped to take cumulative sales of the Beetle through the 4,000,000 mark by the end of the calendar year.

There were changes afoot, however. First of all, for 1961, the Beetle engine was at long last redesigned or, more correctly, replaced with a version of the new engine introduced on the Type 2 range a year earlier. No longer, except for the fact that it was still an air-cooled flat-four design, could the unit be compared with that first seen in the Kübelwagen and Schwimmwagen back in the 1940s. The new engine shared nothing with its predecessor, other than its capacity: 1192cc. A new crankcase, crankshaft, camshaft, cylinders, pistons, cylinder heads, fuel pump and cooling system all helped make this latest engine a more robust unit which also happened to produce more power: 34bhp as opposed to 30bhp. And, although that may not seem a huge improvement in modern terms, as a percentage it represented an increase of over 13 per cent – a useful gain on such a low-power vehicle.

© VOLKSWAGEN OF AMERICA, INC.

How to make a '54 look like a '64.

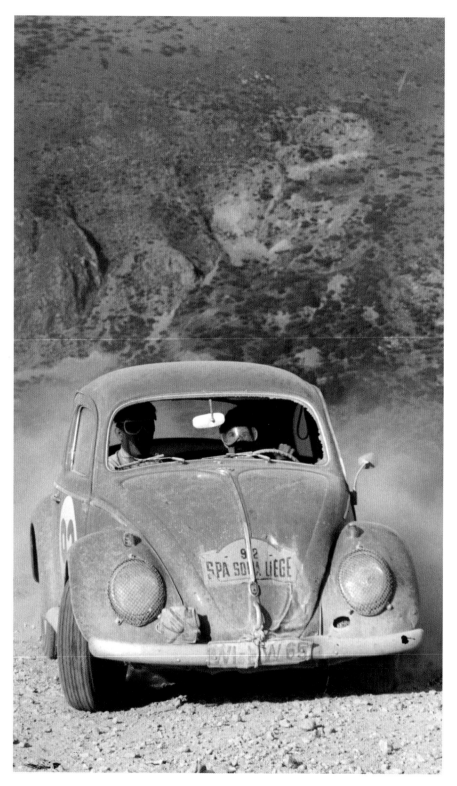

Left Hans Wehner rallied his 1200 Beetle around Europe with great success in the early 1960s, and VW used its exploits extensively in period advertising. In the 1962 Spa-Sofia-Liège rally the crew donned motorcycle goggles after the windscreen was shattered!

More Changes

In addition to the revised engine, a new transmission made its appearance. This was a totally new design, with a one-piece casing as opposed to the old "split-case" transaxle which had been in use relatively unchanged since the late 1940s. The new transmission benefitted from having synchromesh on all forward gears, making it far more pleasant to use, especially in traffic where, on the old model, first gear could only be selected at rest. With a stronger casing, the new design proved to be longer lasting and remained in production, essentially unchanged, until the 1980s.

There were several other modifications made to the Beetle at the same time, including, much to the passenger's delight, the fitting of a second sun visor as standard. The fuel tank was also redesigned and, although having a larger capacity, its improved shape actually resulted in an increase in available luggage space under the boot lid.

In the following year, Volkswagen was somewhat more restrained in its programme of continuous improvement, with the biggest news being a redesigned rear-light cluster,

which now featured a larger lens area with a separate amber turn signal located at the top. The boot lid finally lost its troublesome over-centre stay, which had been fitted to all Beetles since the very beginning. This had been the cause of many damaged bonnets as petrol station attendants tried to shut them without first releasing the stay. A pair of heavy springs now did the job of holding the boot lid open.

Perhaps the most useful improvement was the fitting of a fuel gauge on the dashboard alongside the speedometer, the old floor-mounted reserve tap at last disappearing – except on the standard models. The latter Beetles were rather idiosyncratic in that they still made use of the old 30bhp engine, and came with cable-operated brakes and the customary lack of trim. Although not a big seller by this time, the standard model was to remain on offer for several years to come.

The big news, however, was not to do with the Beetle, but a new model called the Type 3. First announced in September 1961, the new car, which would be sold as the VW 1500, appeared to share little with the Beetle. A new engine – again a development of the unit now used in the Type 2 – was all new, with a swept volume of some 1498cc. The body was far more conventional in styling terms (compared with the Beetle, at least), being what is today known as a "three-box" design and came to be nicknamed the "Notchback". Ever ones to prove they knew how to get the most into the least, Wolfsburg's stylists bestowed upon the Type 3 the unique feature of front and rear luggage compartments. To achieve this, the Type 2 engine was redesigned, with a new cooling system that allowed the engine to be fitted under the floor of the rear luggage area, the cooling fan now being driven from the end of the crankshaft rather than off the generator.

The arrival of the Type 3 on the scene was a very timely development, for the Beetle was having trouble maintaining its lead in the sales stakes. Its market share was down by some 8 per cent at a time when total vehicle sales in Germany were up by over 10 per cent. Although Volkswagen could still boast that it retained a third of the domestic market, out-selling its nearest rival by a factor of two-to-one, the overall trend for the company was downwards and market share would drop below 30 per cent the following year.

One interesting – and troublesome – chapter in Volkswagen's history finally came to a close in October 1961, when a settlement was made to those people who had taken advantage of Hitler's KdF saving scheme over 20 years earlier. The case was first brought to court by a group of savers, led by Karl Stolz, as far back as January 1950. Stolz argued that it was not the fault of those people who had joined the

KdF savings scheme that they had lost all their money after the war. He believed, as did his many followers, that Volkswagen had a moral obligation to repay the money in one form or another, either as a direct rebate or in the form of a discount against the purchase of a new Beetle. Volkswagen management maintained that the present company had no connection whatsoever with the pre-war system and could not be held responsible, either morally or legally, for their conduct.

Legal Complications

At the first court hearing, the judge rejected the savers' claim on the basis that the whole KdF scheme had been nothing but Nazi propaganda. The case went before the supreme court and, while the decision was not totally reversed, there was the feeling that Volkswagen might be considered a partner to the original scheme. Unsure of what the future might hold, Nordhoff took the bull by the horns and sought a more precise ruling on the case. This time Volkswagen was found to be "guilty" and ordered to pay the court costs.

However, that was not the end of things, for in 1954 more evidence was brought before the court and a judgement made that, while Volkswagen was not a partner, it was a responsible party and could therefore be sued by the savers. The following year, the state court then overturned that ruling! The savings

group considered whether to accept a compromise when the factory made an offer of DM250 cash or a credit of DM500 against the purchase of a new Beetle. This was turned down and the savers returned to the supreme court, only to have the case referred back to the lower courts once again.

Finally, in 1961, the case came to an end when the courts ruled that Volkswagen should make cash repayments of between DM25 and DM100, or a credit of between DM150 and DM600 against a new car, depending on how many stamps the saver had in his book. It would be another nine years before the last payments were made, honouring over 120,000 KdF saving contracts, of which just over a half of the claimants opted to buy a new car. While all this continued, the number of surviving claimants had obviously started to shrink, but the total cost to the company was in excess of DM34 million, either in cash or credit – the up-side being that with this ruling the last remaining ghost from the political past had finally been laid to rest.

Rising Production

The end of 1962 would see a leap to a production run of some 1,004,338 vehicles, while the 1,000,000th Beetle was sold in the USA. America had become such a large and important market that Volkswagen opened a new headquarters there, at Englewood Cliffs in New Jersey,

on 20 November 1962. In hindsight, it is perhaps a little surprising that the company never opened a manufacturing plant in North America specifically to assemble the Beetle, considering how many of them were sold there. Many years later, a VW plant would be built in Westmoreland, Pennsylvania, to assemble the Rabbit, the US version of the best-selling front-engined Golf, but it was destined to close after a troubled history.

The 1963 Beetles differed little from their predecessor, with the exception of an improved heating system – the new "fresh-air" system was designed to prevent engine fumes from entering the car, while controls under the back seat regulated the flow of warm air to the rear passenger compartment. One small cosmetic detail was the removal of the enamelled Wolfsburg crest from the front boot lid, a sad loss in the eyes of many enthusiasts who saw it as a link with a historic past.

The 1964 Beetle was essentially little different from the 1963 model, with one notable exception: the fabric folding sunroof, which had been available since 1950, finally made way for a far more sophisticated steel sliding roof on the export models. Standard Beetles, however, retained the fabric roof. The steering wheel was redesigned to incorporate a simple two-thumb horn push which replaced the semi-circular design introduced four years earlier. Other details included larger front indicators and plain chromed hubcaps –

no longer would the VW logo be picked out in black. A total of 1,216,390 Beetles were built that calendar year, another production record that proved the VW was as popular as ever.

A Clearer View

However, there were big changes afoot for 1965, with another major redesign of the bodywork taking place in the form of slimmer body pillars and a slightly curved windscreen. The effect of these modifications was to make the overall glass area noticeably larger than the old model, with the rear window alone being some 10mm (0.39in) wider and 20mm (0.79in) deeper than before. The windscreen was 28mm (1.1in) taller, too. The opening quarter lights in the doors changed shape, with their pillars being raked back at a slight angle to give the car a more modern look. At the rear, the familiar T-handle engine-lid lock made way for a plain push-button latch (which still could not be locked).

More Power

Inside the 1965 model there were new heater control levers which replaced the old rotary knob which had been used since October 1952. The right-hand lever turned the heating system on while the left-hand one opened or shut the vents under the rear seat. While these changes may have made the Beetle an altogether better car, it was beginning to struggle to stay in the limelight and many dealers must have prayed for something new to tell their customers. Rival manufacturers might not have been able to boast of matching the VW's reliability but they could argue that their cars were more modern, more powerful and more enjoyable to drive. It was difficult not to agree with them, despite the fact that the Beetle's sales figures continued to impress: in the USA, for example, over 295,000 were sold that year. What was needed was more than a cosmetic change if the Beetle was to stay ahead of the competition.

Their prayers were answered when, in August 1965, Volkswagen launched the 1300 Beetle, powered by a 1285cc engine using the 69mm (2.72in) crankshaft from the 1500 Type 3 model. The result was an increase in horsepower from 34bhp to 40bhp, a gain of some 17.6 per cent. To distinguish the new model from others, there was a discreet "1300" badge on the engine lid, while a new style of wheel, with ventilation slots around the hubcap, was borrowed from the Type 3 range. A flat hubcap was also fitted, although the familiar domed design remained in use on the 1200cc standard versions.

These 1966 models also featured a re-designed front suspension system, where the original king- and link-pin design was replaced with a more modern ball-joint set-up. At the same time, the number and size of torsion leaves in the front axle beam was changed to improve the ride quality. The result was a car that was far more pleasant to drive and which had a better chance of keeping up with other traffic – the top speed of the 1300 Beetle was a mighty 121km/h (75mph). Although total Beetle production was slightly down at 1,021,298, sales in the vital US market were up by just under 6,000 to 302,423 in 1966.

For 1967, Volkswagen had some big changes in store, all aimed at keeping the Beetle at the top of the sales charts. There was a new model introduced in the form of the 1500 Beetle, which used a revised version of the 44bhp Type 3 engine and came with disc brakes fitted to the front axle. Well, they were fitted to European models, but the US market inexplicably had to put up with the old drum brakes. For some reason, no Beetle would ever be offered in the USA with disc brakes. However, while the Europeans still had to suffer six-volt electrics, the US-bound VWs were sold with 12-volt systems.

The new 1500 model is generally thought to be the best Beetle ever to be offered, with superior performance, stopping power and handling, thanks to a new "Z-bar", or equalizer spring, incorporated into the rear suspension. American models even came with "upright" sealed-beam headlamps (taken once again from the Type 3) which greatly improved visibility at night, although European Beetles retained the traditional sloping headlamps for another year. The 1300 Beetle continued to be offered alongside the new model but did not benefit from the improved braking system, while the old 1200 engine was still available in what became known as the 1300A. In January 1967, a new basic Beetle was introduced, called the *Sparkäfer*, or "Economy Beetle". Based on the 1300 model, this bottom-of-the-range Beetle was something of a modern version of the old standard model with basic trim, little chrome and few home comforts. It was intended to help bolster flagging sales.

The 1967 Beetle model range was an expensive exercise for Volkswagen as there were numerous parts that were exclusive to the model. The engine lid, for example, had to be redesigned to accommodate the new engine, which in turn meant a new rear valance had to be fitted. The door handles, both inside and out, were also unique, being redesigned yet again at the end of the model year. Today, the '67s are sought after by enthusiasts as they represent the best of the "old" style of VW, for 1968 models were, again, very different.

Changes Abound

The most obvious change for '68 was the introduction of heavy "Euro" bumpers designed to meet the more stringent American safety regulations. These clumsy bumpers, while keeping the safety experts happy, did little to enhance the steadily changing appearance of the Beetle. Other improvements made by Wolfsburg included yet another engine lid, this time considerably shorter and more square in design than its predecessor, and an externally-mounted fuel filler. New door handles with trigger levers, aimed at preventing the door from bursting open in a roll-over accident, and a collapsible steering column were further safety features. All models now came with the Type 3's upright headlamps, along with a new design of rear light unit on all but the basic Beetle. As far as the running gear was concerned, the old five-bolt style of wheel fitting, in use since the very first KdF-Wagens, finally gave way to a more rigid four-bolt design. But perhaps the biggest improvement of all, on European models, was the introduction of a 12-volt electrical system to bring them in line with their US-specification counterparts.

Perhaps the most technically interesting Beetle to date was introduced this year, the so-called "semi-automatic". This was a 1500 model equipped with a unique three-speed transmission that allowed the driver to change gear without the use of a clutch. In fact, thanks to a torque converter, the car could be started and driven from rest in any gear. This new model accounted for half of all sales of 1500 Beetles in the first four months of production.

Aside from the transmission, the semi-automatic also featured a far superior rear suspension system, with semi-trailing arms and double-jointed halfshafts. At last, Volkswagen appeared to acknowledge that the old swing-axle design had its shortcomings, so much so, in fact, that all Beetles destined for sale in the USA came with the IRS suspension regardless of the type of transmission used. These US-specification models also came with a 1600cc engine. Once again, one has to question why only the US market got such preferential treatment when it would have been more cost-effective for the factory to produce the same models for all markets.

End Of An Era

In 1968, Heinz Nordhoff, who had led the Volkswagen organization since the late 1940s, suffered a heart attack and died. Throughout his life at Wolfsburg, Nordhoff had been held in high esteem, credited with being the person responsible for ensuring the success of the Beetle. Indeed, Ferdinand Porsche, viewing the production line at Wolfsburg, once turned to Nordhoff and said "You know, Herr Nordhoff, this is the way I always imagined it, but I didn't know I was right until you proved it". There could be no finer epitaph for the man who made Porsche's dream a reality, from the man himself.

Nordhoff had many critics, people who felt the company's reliance on just one model for so long would damage future prospects. Tired of such criticisms, Nordhoff on one occasion gathered together all the design exercises that had been considered throughout the 1950s and early 1960s in an effort to prove that still waters do indeed run deep. However, they could not disguise the fact that Nordhoff's baby, the Type 3, had not been the success he had hoped. There was no getting away from the point that, although the Beetle's days as the number one bestseller were numbered, it refused to lie down and die. Indeed, in 1968, American sales reached another all-time high, with some 390,000 Beetles being sold in the USA.

New Models?

Nordhoff's successor was Kurt Lotz, who quickly realized that the company had been too successful throughout the 1960s to risk making any sudden changes to the way it was run. However, he did hint at change in the future, with the occasional remark suggesting that new models might be around the corner. One thing that Lotz was well aware of was Volkswagen's heavy dependence on the American market. Following the revaluation of the Deutschmark, Lotz was worried that this would mean a damaging rise in vehicle prices abroad, so he opted to absorb much of the increase, aware of the threat of pressure from other importers – especially those from the Far East. However, some other decisions made while he was in control did the company fewer favours: the Type 4 range was launched in August 1968 and proved to be one of the biggest disappointments in Volkswagen history. Heavy, underpowered and too expensive, the 411 and the later 412 were never the success Lotz had hoped. Had it been launched five years earlier, things might have been different but, as the Americans say, it was a day late and a dollar short.

However, the last months of the decade were not all doom and gloom, for on 29 November 1969 Volkswagen celebrated the assembly of the 15,000,000th vehicle since the war and in December announced the formation of a new Swedish import company, Svenska Volkswagen AB, which took over from the old Scania-Vabis concern, which had handled the business since the 1950s.

Looking back over the decade, Volkswagen witnessed some major events in the Beetle's life. First there was the new engine and transmission, followed by no fewer than three revised body designs and the introduction of an interesting semi-automatic model. Then, of course, there was the Type 3 range, which included a crisply styled Karmann Ghia version, a revised Type 2 in 1967 and finally the heavyweight, and ultimately unsuccessful, Type 4. Taking stock of all these developments, it is hard to point a finger at Nordhoff and accuse him of adopting a one-model policy. The Volkswagen range entered the 1970s with a quite staggering variety of vehicles, from the basic 1200 *Sparkäfer* to a four-door, fuel-injected family saloon.

It had become clear, early on in the decade, that the Wolfsburg site would not be able to cope with future production. In view of this, Volkswagen opened a number of factories around the world. There had been an assembly plant in Mexico since 1954 (the current plant was opened in 1967 at Puebla, 120km/75 miles south-east of Mexico City), along with others in Brazil, Belgium, Ireland, South Africa, Australia, New Zealand and the Philippines, all established in the 1950s. In 1961 these were joined by one in Uruguay, then Venezuela in 1963, Portugal in 1964, Peru in 1966 and Malaysia and Singapore in 1968. In addition, there were no fewer than three factories, including Wolfsburg, in Germany: Emden had opened its gates in December 1964 and then, of course, there was Osnabrück, site of the Karmann factory, where Karmann Ghias and Beetle cabriolets continued to be produced and which had started Beetle production in 1949. In addition, Type 2s were built at Hanover.

As a world car, the Volkswagen had arrived, but by now, the name was no longer associated solely with the Beetle. •

Right The Disney *Herbie* movies introduced the Beetle to a whole new generation.

1968: Herbie

Volkswagen Press (0908) 601187

improving the breed

By the start of the 1970s, it was evident that, if it was to remain as Volkswagen's number one product, the Beetle was in dire need of a redesign. The dilemma here, as far as Volkswagen was concerned, was that any improvements which might make the Beetle a more marketable product would almost certainly be in conflict with the whole *raison d'être* of the model. The Beetle had always sold because it was perceived to be an inexpensive, honest motor car with few frills and no gimmicks. By "improving" the product, the company ran the risk of compromising this honesty which had long been the Beetle's strongest selling point.

However, by now there were fewer diehard Beetle owners – people who would automatically buy a Beetle no matter what other options might be open to them. There was a new generation of customers, who had grown up in the more affluent 1960s, for whom the no-nonsense appeal of the Beetle was not enough to sway their purchasing decisions. If it was inexpensive transport they were seeking, then there were several other companies which offered cheap alternatives: the Renault 4, NSU Prinz, even the British Mini.

With the continuing production of the Type 3 models, a steadily revised Type 2 range, the introduction of the unwieldy Type 4 and links with the NSU-Audi empire, Volkswagen had what was, on the surface, a very impressive line-up. However, the top-selling model was still the Beetle, and its fortunes were starting to slip. What was the answer? According to Kurt Lotz and his successor – in October 1971 – Rudolph Leiding, the solution was a "new" Beetle. Perhaps it would also be fair to say, a new water-cooled car as well: the K70.

But the K70 was a disaster for Volkswagen. Conceived as an NSU and inherited by Volkswagen when it acquired the Neckarsülm company in 1969, the K70 was something new as far as VW was concerned. The angular three-box saloon was powered by an in-line, front-mounted water-cooled engine which drove the front wheels via a transaxle unit. Loosely based on the old NSU air-cooled engine, the K70's powerplant produced 100bhp from its 1700cc. Several pundits at the time questioned the wisdom of Volkswagen marketing a car which was so close in size and price to the existing Type 4 models, but VW ignored such comments. In hindsight, it is easy to suggest that instead of one millstone round its neck, Wolfsburg now had two to contend with.

A Costly Error?

The K70 proved to be an expensive and unwise diversion as far as Volkswagen's long-term future was concerned. The car was never a success, despite massive pre-launch publicity and a sales drive which proclaimed it as the way ahead in automotive design. The appalling aerodynamics (a Cd figure of 0.51 – when even the Beetle's was only 0.44!) resulted in poor fuel economy, while it cost so much to build that it could never be a profitable model for the company. Indeed, as a whole, Volkswagen's profits fell by over 40 per cent at this time and Kurt Lotz was considered to be largely to blame for this downturn in the company's fortunes – although it has to be said that this was a period when there was considerable financial upheaval in Western Europe as a whole.

With few changes to the Beetle for the 1970 model year, many potential customers delayed buying a new car in the hope that the new year would see some sign of change. Many Europeans felt disappointed that they had been denied the introduction of the IRS (independent rear suspension) system enjoyed by the Americans since 1968. True, it did seem illogical to build one car for the USA and another for the domestic market, but VW appeared adamant initially that there was no need to introduce the new suspension design closer to home.

Despite offering a variety of engine and model combinations, such as a 1200 with the 1300 engine, or a 1300 with a 1200 engine as well as the 1500, with either manual or semi-automatic transmission, Wolfsburg's 1970 line-up looked little different to previous models. However, 1971 was to change all that.

Introduced to the world as the Super Beetle, the 1302 and 1302S models were heralded as being the ultimate development of the People's Car. The former was powered by a development of the old 1300 engine, now equipped with all-new dual-port cylinder heads with separate inlet ports for each cylinder (all previous cylinder heads used a single siamesed inlet port) which produced 44bhp, while the latter came with a new 1600cc engine producing 50bhp. To help overcome the long-term problem of the oil cooler blocking the cooling airflow to number three cylinder (this was always the most likely to seize), the engine shrouding was redesigned and the oil cooler was now mounted externally and fed by extra ductwork.

New Suspension

The new engine was a revelation and remains one of the best ever fitted to the Beetle. It was not only more powerful and more torquey, but also – in theory at least – more reliable, with a redesigned crankcase and improved oil system. However, the most interesting aspect of the new models could be found underneath that familiar bodywork: not only was the previously US-only

Right The 1970s saw Volkswagen drastically revamp their model line-up, but the Type 4 and the K70 were poorly conceived. The NSU-designed K70 was technically flawed, and became an expensive failure.

IRS suspension system finally made available to Europeans, but there was an all-new front suspension design, too. Forsaking Ferdinand Porsche's beloved torsion-bar design, which had been in use since the very first prototypes built before World War II, Volkswagen engineers adopted an advanced MacPherson strut front suspension system which considerably changed the whole handling characteristics of the Beetle. The system was similar to that which had been used on the Type 4 range since its introduction three years earlier, and was coming into widespread use across the rest of the industry.

The new front suspension also allowed the designers to increase the luggage-carrying capacity, as the boot could be made deeper and wider, with the spare wheel now being laid down flat in front of a relocated fuel tank. The result was a massive increase in volume, from just under 0.14m³ (5cu ft) to a little over 0.25m³ (9cu ft). Add this to the space that had always been available behind the rear seat and, more than 30 years after it was designed, the Beetle suddenly became a true family car with a worthwhile carrying capacity.

While the new engine and suspension specification may have brought a smile to the face of many potential customers, the revised styling did little to endear the 1302 and 1302S models to the dyed-in-the-wool enthusiast. Taking advantage of the new front suspension, the stylists saw fit to make the nose of the new models somewhat fatter, more bulbous and hence more capacious than their predecessors. However, the redesign, although subtle as far as the casual observer was concerned, required not only new inner wings to accommodate the MacPherson strut suspension, but also a new spare-wheel well, fuel tank mounting panel, wings, bonnet and front valance. Other areas of the bodyshell were revised, with a new through-flow ventilation system, with

vents let into the rear quarter-panels behind the rear-side windows, and a redesigned engine cover adding to the new look. The floorpan was all-new, too, making this by far the most extensive – and costly – revision of the Beetle to be undertaken since it was first launched.

No 1 In America

With hindsight, it is questionable whether the expenditure was worth it for, with the introduction of the K70, the writing appeared to be on the wall for the air-cooled Volkswagen. Or was it? Certainly sales in the USA continued a downward trend from 366,790 in 1970 to 331,191 in 1971,

and there were no signs of a U-turn. However, the Beetle remained the number one imported car in North America. In spite of the downturn in sales, the factory continued to develop the Beetle still further, as well as offering the basic 1200 and 1300 Beetles in Europe with their torsion-bar front suspension and swing-axle rear end.

Another New Face

In October 1971, Kurt Lotz stepped down as head of Volkswagen, to be replaced by Rudolph Leiding, who had cut his teeth with Volkswagen back in the early Nordhoff days, acting as deputy in the service department until 1958, when he was put in charge of the Kassel plant, which assembled transmissions. After a spell with the ailing Auto-Union company, Leiding was then appointed head of VW do Brazil, the South American manufacturing facility that had been set up by Nordhoff's longtime ally, Friedrich Schultz-Wenk. He eventually arrived in Wolfsburg at a time when some serious rethinking was necessary, not only as far as the Beetle was concerned, but for the range as a whole.

The new-look Beetle remained pretty much unchanged for 1972.

The rear windscreen was enlarged by 40mm (1.57in), top to bottom, while the through-flow ventilation vents were modified to prevent water from getting into the car while stationary. The engine lid was redesigned with four sets of vents, in place of two and, as a consequence, the drainage tray, which had been fitted to prevent rain from entering the engine compartment, was deleted. To prevent any problems with water soaking the electrical system, Volkswagen improved the damp-proofing of the distributor and coil.

There were other less obvious changes, too. For example, the door-handle trigger releases were made longer, necessitating a modification to the door panel itself. Bumper mountings were altered, the steering wheel and switchgear redesigned, the body mountings were changed slightly, the lock on the engine lid modified – all were considered necessary by the Volkswagen engineers, but one has to question, yet again, the wisdom of such minor redesigning when they must have realized there was yet another "new" Beetle on the way.

The greatest news of all for Volkswagen in 1972 was that on 17 February, the Beetle finally became the biggest-selling car of all time, with sales totalling 15,007,034 – which took the title away from the Ford Model T, the remarkable vehicle which had been a source of inspiration to both Ferdinand Porsche and Adolf Hitler so many years before.

VW marked this occasion with the launch of a special Marathon edition. And another milestone was passed in October when the 3,000,000th exchange engine was produced by the Kassel plant. The old and overweight 411 range was phased out, making way for the sharper-looking 412 models, but they did not match up to Volkswagen's sales department's expectations either.

A Whole New Look

The new 1973 model year saw the ever-changing face of the Beetle undergo yet further alteration, by far the biggest ever. The result was the 1303 range which, unlike any previous Beetles, came with a deep, panoramic, curved windscreen. This major change of direction was partly to allow more interior space for the front-seat passengers, as the dashboard could now be mounted further away. The traditional plain metal dashboard made way for one with plenty of padding, giving greater protection for the occupants of the car in the event of an accident. The instruments were now housed in a separate binnacle directly in front of the driver, while a totally revised ventilation and demisting system helped keep the passengers cool in summer and the windscreen clear in winter.

Further Changes

In addition to the radical restyling of the windscreen and scuttle panel, the roof was made less curved and the rear wings redesigned. These were changed to accommodate all-new rear light assemblies which were soon nick-named "elephant's feet" because of their large, round shape. For many purists, this extensive revamp of Ferdinand Porsche's brainchild was one step too far and there are many who consider the 1303 models to be the least attractive Beetles of all. However, those with a less blinkered outlook can rightly claim that the 1303 range – particularly the 1600cc 1303S – was the best that Volkswagen had ever offered, with the most powerful engines, the most sophisticated suspension, the most interior space, the best heating and ventilation system, disc brakes, excellent luggage capacity and a good build quality. But was it still a Beetle? After all, wasn't the Beetle supposed to be a basic means of transport for the masses?

During 1973, there were several revisions made to the model range, including the Economy Beetle (the old *Sparkäfer*) which was now fitted with the large new rear lights from the 1303 model and black-painted Euro bumpers. There was a 1200L model which, as the title suggests, was a de luxe version of the basic flat-screen Beetle with chromed bumpers, better interior trim, reversing lights and a choice of either the 34bhp 1200 or 44bhp 1300 engines. Both the 1303 and 1303S could be ordered with the "L" specification, offering a higher standard of trim throughout, but there was also a 1303A for the home market which was a low-spec Super Beetle with the 1200 engine.

Special Models

This was an era when Volkswagen tried various marketing tactics in an effort to rekindle interest in the Beetle ahead of the launch of the new water-cooled range the following year. First there was the Yellow and Black Racer model which was nothing more than a 1303S with yellow bodywork, black bonnet and engine lid, 5.5J x 15 sports wheels with 175/70 tyres and black bumpers. Later the same year, in preparation for the 1974 season, Volkswagen announced the Big Beetle which was a 1303S with the same sports wheel and tyre combination, black stripes along the bottoms of the doors and a "1303 Big" decal.

Then there was the crazy, but immensely popular, Jeans Beetle, which was a basic 1200 in deep yellow with a denim interior designed to look like a pair of Levi's jeans. Blacked-out body-trim and bumpers helped keep the cost to a minimum. The Jeans model, although nothing more than an inexpensive marketing exercise, has proved to be one of the most enduring of all late-model Beetles. Original versions are still quite sought-after, as the denim upholstery material wore badly in daily use and was often replaced with the regular black vinyl trim.

There were few major changes to the specification of 1974 models compared with that of the previous year's. For the USA, the bumper mountings were changed to a shock-absorbing design, to keep abreast of the latest safety regulations which required that a car be able to withstand an 8km/h (5mph) impact without sustaining damage. There were also a number of minor improvements made to the engine, including twin pre-heat pipes on the inlet manifold, modified carburettor, a redesigned exhaust system and new heat exchangers, but that was all. However, there were other changes afoot and an important new arrival on the scene.

Water-Cooled Cousins

In March 1974, the Volkswagen Scirocco was launched, followed closely by the Golf in May. The latter was a small family hatchback, powered by a transversely-mounted, four-cylinder, water-cooled engine driving the front wheels. A far cry from the poorly conceived K70, the Golf and its more sporting Scirocco stable-mate soon earned favourable reviews from the motoring press. Many even went so far as to suggest that this was indeed the end of the road for the Beetle. After all, the Golf offered superior performance, greater interior space and superior luggage-carrying capacity. It was also faster, more fuel-efficient and no more expensive to buy.

The saddest news of all in 1974 was the announcement that, on 1 July, the very last Beetle would roll off the assembly line at Wolfsburg. However, the good news was that production would continue at the Emden plant where all US-specification Beetles had been built since the end of 1964, although the bodyshells continued to be produced at Wolfsburg. Since the end of the war, a total of 11,916,519 Beetles had been built at the original Volkswagen factory.

For 1975, there were changes afoot at Wolfsburg, for Rudolph Leiding resigned his chairmanship of Volkswagen AG on 10 January. One month later, Tony Schmücker, a member of the company's advisory committee, was appointed chairman. The Beetle range was now reduced considerably, as the factory acknowledged the shift in demand in the marketplace. Most of the changes seen this year were made for reasons of economy, such as fitting small plastic dust caps instead of real metal hubcaps on the 1200 models. There was no glove box lid, either. The front indicators were now incorporated into the front bumpers across the range, perversely placing them where they are at their most vulnerable to parking damage. The 1303 range – now simply badged as "1303" regardless of engine size or trim specification – did, however, benefit from the fitting of a rack-and-pinion steering system in place of the old steering box.

Fuel-Injection

The big news on the American market was the introduction of fuel-injection on the Beetle engine in an effort to meet ever-more stringent exhaust emission regulations. The system, manufactured by Robert Bosch, was a relatively simple design, with a fuel loop ("ring main") which supplied the injector units with fuel at a constant pressure. The injectors were triggered by a second set of contact points in the distributor. The system worked well but did little to improve either the performance or the fuel economy of the Beetle. Models with this Bosch system installed could be identified by the single exhaust tailpipe and the "Fuel Injection" badge on the engine lid. To accommodate the redesigned exhaust system, a new rear valance was fitted – this appeared on all models, regardless of whether an injection engine was fitted or not.

Back To Basics

For the Beetle, this was almost the end of the road as far as further development was concerned. On 31 July 1975, the last 1303s came off the production line at Emden, to leave just the basic 1200 models to keep the Beetle going in saloon form.

Even the 1300 engine option was dropped from the line-up. The curved windscreen did, however, continue to be a feature of the cabriolet models which were still being built at Osnabrück by Karmann. Most of these were destined to cross the Atlantic, where sales of convertible cars remained steady.

In Europe, the customer could only buy a Beetle with swing-axle rear suspension, torsion-bar front and a 1200 engine, although a 1600 could be supplied to order. The Beetle now seemed very much down the list of Volkswagen's priorities, on home territory at least. Abroad, a new factory in Lagos, Nigeria, opened in March 1975 to assemble Beetles at the rate of 60 each day. In Mexico, 550 cars a day were being built at the Puebla factory.

Sales in America showed a marked downward trend in 1975, not so much due to any loss of interest in the product, but because the factory dramatically cut back production. In fact, a total of only 267,815 Beetles were built in calendar year 1975, as opposed to 818,456 the previous year. Of these, just 82,030 were sold in the USA as opposed to 344,177 in 1972, 350,357 in 1973 and 226,098 in 1974. To try and appeal to the public, a special edition "La Grande Bug" was sold in the USA in the 1975 model year, the demand for which was so great that a second and third series had to be built. However, for the first time ever, Volkswagen lost the title of number one exporter to

Left Launched in 1974, the new water-cooled, front-wheel-drive Golf effectively spelt the end for Beetle production at Wolfsburg. It would also go on to be a world-beater.

the USA, that claim now being made by the Japanese.

There were no changes made for 1976, except that it was no longer possible to buy a Beetle with a six-volt electrical system. Yes, until August 1976, the basic model Beetle was still available on some markets with the old-style electrical system! By this time, even the simple matter of buying a spare six-volt headlamp bulb would have been a problem in some places, let alone trying to find a new radio for your basic Beetle. Apart from this revelation, there were two other landmarks to give cause for celebration at Wolfsburg: the 1,000,000th Golf and the 30,000,000th Volkswagen were produced in 1976. The year's total Beetle production was just 176,287, of which only 26,794 found their way to the USA. The writing was on the wall for what was cumulatively still the world's best-selling car, despite the introduction on the US market of the attractive "Triple White" special edition cabriolet with its white paintwork, white hood and white interior trim.

There were to be few changes made in 1977, and it was announced in the USA that this was the last year that a saloon model would be available. The decision caused much sadness among Volkswagen fans in America, although they could console themselves with the fact that they could still buy a cabriolet. With just 101,292 Beetles built to satisfy the whole world, it is not surprising that

American sales dropped still further to 19,245 that year.

End Of The Line

On 19 January 1978, the last Beetle saloon to be built on German soil left the assembly line at Emden, although the cabriolet continued to be built at the Karmann coachworks, still in 1303 curved-windscreen format. Instead, all future Beetles would be imported into Germany from the Mexico factory and built to the current Mexican specification. This included the trusty 34bhp 1200 engine, torsion-bar front suspension, swing-axle rear, flat windscreen and a smaller rear window like those used on German models between 1965 and 1971. At least the "old" window now featured a heating element. The Mexican Beetles appeared to be less austere than the last of the European-produced cars, with chrome hubcaps and trim, radial tyres, inertia reel seat belts, anti-dazzle mirror and adjustable head restraints. However, there was no longer the option of the more powerful 50bhp 1600 engine.

Swan Song

In the USA, the second of a series of special "Champagne" models was launched. These were first sold in 1977 to celebrate, of all things, the sale of 1,000,000 Golfs, or Rabbits as they were known in the USA. While this was a milestone that probably

held little interest as far as the Beetle owner was concerned, the resultant special edition cabriolet was much sought-after at the time and remains so to this day. The specification included special paintwork in Red Metallic or Ancona Blue Metallic, an ivory-coloured hood and interior trim, wood-panelled dashboard, quartz clock, whitewall tyres and sports wheels. There was even a heated rear window fitted to the folding roof. Just two were offered to each dealer, and many took this to mean that this was the Beetle's swan-song in the USA. And it very nearly was.

In 1979 there would be no further changes made to the Beetle, although once again there would be a special edition cabriolet sold on the American market. This was the "Epilog" (sic) which was supplied in Henry Ford's favourite colour scheme of any colour you like as long as it's black. This time there was only one issued to each dealer and it really was the Beetle's swan song for the US market, as the Mexican-built Beetles were never "Federalized" so as to be legal for sale in North America. They met neither the emission nor safety regulations current in the USA and remained a dream as far as American enthusiasts were concerned.

Finally, on 10 January 1980, the very last Beetle cabriolet drove off the production line at Karmann and straight into the factory museum to take pride of place. There had been 331,850 cabriolets built since

production began in 1949, with by far the greatest number finding their way to the USA. It was a black day indeed for Volkswagen fans the world over, for this meant that no longer was it possible to buy a Beetle that had been assembled anywhere in Europe.

Production still continued apace in many places throughout the world, however, with Mexico remaining the source of all new Beetles as far as Germany was concerned. The model was still being assembled in Peru, Uruguay, Brazil, Venezuela, Nigeria, the Philippines and, until 1979, South Africa. It is ironic that, when the factory management made the decision to stop building the Beetle in Germany in 1978, domestic sales rose by some 55 per cent as the humbly specced Mexican version became available. Perhaps it was a sign that the customer really had not been impressed with all the MacPherson strut suspension, IRS rear ends, bulbous windscreens, fancy ventilation systems and seemingly endless gimmicky special editions. Perhaps all he wanted was a basic, reliable, no-fuss Beetle, just like the one he used to be able to buy. Or perhaps it was just a hint of nostalgia... After all, it always seems to be human nature to want something you can't have any more.●

the latin connection

With Beetle production finally halted in Europe, all eyes turned towards South America. Sales prospects here still looked good – the poor road systems and lack of adequate public transport suggested that there was a large potential market for a ruggedly built, low-cost vehicle in South America. Government support was also available to help finance the enterprise. At Puebla, in Mexico, an assembly plant had first been established in 1954, when just 500 Beetles were built from CKD kits (CKD = Completely Knocked Down – i.e. an entire car supplied in component form). The policy of supplying CKD Beetles was to prove popular for Volkswagen as it was a way in which its products could be imported into certain countries without flouting local trade restrictions. Several countries had, by now, imposed a limit on imports in an effort to encourage local industry and thereby bolster their flagging post-war economies.

Mexican-assembled Beetles proved popular on the home market, with sales growing steadily throughout the 1950s. Their success, however, attracted the attention of the Mexican government which, fearing that too much money was being siphoned out of the economy, ordered that in future all Mexican-built cars were to have a higher local content. As a result of this pressure, Volkswagen de Mexico increased the percentage of locally made components to 60 per cent in 1962.

By 1979, after the last German-built Beetle saloon had left the lines, the Mexican local content was further increased to 71 per cent. As far as market share was concerned, Mexican Beetles accounted for roughly one third of all domestic car sales.

Back To Germany

But Mexican Beetles weren't *only* sold in Mexico. As we have seen, when Beetle production finally came to a halt in Germany, firstly at Wolfsburg and then Emden, Volkswagen made the slightly ironic decision to re-import the car from Mexico. Demand was high, despite the relatively low specification of the Mexican models, which came with the basic 1200cc 34bhp engine, swing-axle rear and torsion-bar front suspension and a flat windscreen. However, the interior trim was slightly improved, with modern chequered upholstery and mildly revised instrumentation. The price was also attractive; it worked out at some 8 per cent less than the last of the German-built Beetles.

Although the overall appearance of the Mexican Beetle was more impressive than the last of the German-assembled examples, with chromed hubcaps and bumpers and an attractive range of colours, the general feeling has always been that they never quite matched up to the quality of the Wolfsburg- or Emden-built cars. Maybe that's nostalgia coming to the fore, or maybe it really was the case. Whatever, for anyone who wished to buy a new Beetle in Europe, there was now only one choice, and it was Mexican, take it or leave it.

20 Million Beetles!

The greatest landmark of all in Volkswagen's history occurred on 15 May 1981, when the 20,000,000th Beetle rolled off the line at Puebla, consolidating its position as the biggest-selling car in motoring history. To celebrate this occasion, a special range of Beetles was offered for sale, each finished in silver with a commemorative plaque proclaiming the new sales record. The following year, on 11 November, the 20,000,000th vehicle to be built at Wolfsburg was completed but, alas, this was not a Beetle but a "new generation" Golf Turbo Diesel.

The Mexican Beetle continued to be sold in Germany, with annual sales exceeding 17,500, until 20 August 1985, when the last shipment arrived. The event was celebrated, for want of a better word, by a series of special "Jubilee" models which were built to mark the 50th anniversary of the Beetle, for it was back in 1935 that the Beetle project had first seen the light of day. Who could ever have expected the humble People's Car to have survived the war, enjoy a long spell as the number one best-selling car of all time and still be on sale half a century later? The Beetle was even

voted "Car Of The Century" by the world's motoring press in 1990, following a survey held by the French magazine, *Auto Moto*. For a while, even when they were no longer available through VW dealerships, Mexican Beetles were still sold in Germany through specialist outlets. They were even available at one point via a chain of supermarkets.

While Beetles continued to be produced in Mexico, another chapter in its remarkable history was about to open. This part of the story really begins 40 years earlier, in 1950, when José Thompson, head of Brasmotor, the Chrysler importer for Brazil, became intrigued by the Beetle and enquired whether he might be able to sell the car in his part of South America. His initial approaches to Wolfsburg were unsuccessful, but his persistence paid off in 1949 when, through his friendship with C.T. Tomaz, head of Chrysler, Thompson was able to establish contact with Heinz Nordhoff. Nordhoff visited Brazil with his colleague, Friedrich Schultz-Wenk. Once there, Nordhoff could not fail to be impressed by Thompson's enthusiasm, or by the potential he recognized in the market, and he agreed to help set up an assembly plant in Brazil.

A New Factory

The first fruit of this liaison was a series of Beetles completed in 1953 at a rented industrial shed in

Ipiranga, a suburb of Sao Paulo, the cars having again been supplied in CKD form from Germany. Between 1953 and 1957, a total of 2,268 Beetles and 552 Type 2s were assembled at Sao Paulo. However, in 1957, permission was granted to build a new factory which would allow full domestic manufacture of Volkswagens, thereby helping the Brazilian economy by reducing the number of imports. Indeed, until this plant was built, Brazil had to rely entirely on imported vehicles. In 1951, for example, the total expenditure on imported cars was some $276,500,000 and the average annual expenditure on vehicle imports during the 1950s was around $130,000,000. Such was the government's concern about the situation that a committee, GEIA (Automobile Industry's Export Group), headed by Lucio Meira, was established in June 1956, with a brief to investigate ways round this imbalance between imports and exports.

That same year, Volkswagen do Brazil began work on building a new 10,000m² (107,600sq ft) assembly plant, located some 23km (14 miles) from Sao Paulo on the Via Anchieta, a road which linked the city with the port of Santos. However, it was not until 2 September the following year that the first vehicle – a Type 2 – was completed, with the first Beetle not seeing the light of day until 3 January 1959. This car was purchased only four days later by Eduardo Matarazzo for the sum of Cr$471,200 from the

Marcas Famosas dealership in Sao Paulo.

Despite having been in operation for almost two years, the plant was not officially opened until 18 November 1959, by President Juscelino Kubitschek and Sao Paulo State Governor, Prof Carvalho Pinto. Also in attendance were Wolfsburg chief, Heinz Nordhoff, and Friedrich Schultz-Wenk, who had been appointed head of Volkswagen do Brazil. Over the next 12 months, some 8,406 Beetles would be sold in Brazil and, by 1962, it had become the country's number-one selling car, with a total of 31,014 units sold. On 4 July 1967, the 500,000th Beetle – or Fusca, as it became officially known in Brazil – was built at the Sao Paulo plant. In line with Brazilian government policy, these domestically built Beetles had a local content of 54 per cent.

New Models

In June 1968, Rudolph Leiding took over the Brazilian factory from Schultz-Wenk and was himself replaced by Werner P. Schmidt in 1971, when he returned to Wolfsburg to oversee the introduction of several new models. During Schmidt's reign, a number of new vehicles were added to the range, including the Brazilian equivalent of the Type 3 sedan, a Variant and in 1970 the so-called Fuscão, a Beetle with a larger 1500cc engine. Later, Schmidt would add the sporting Type 4-engined

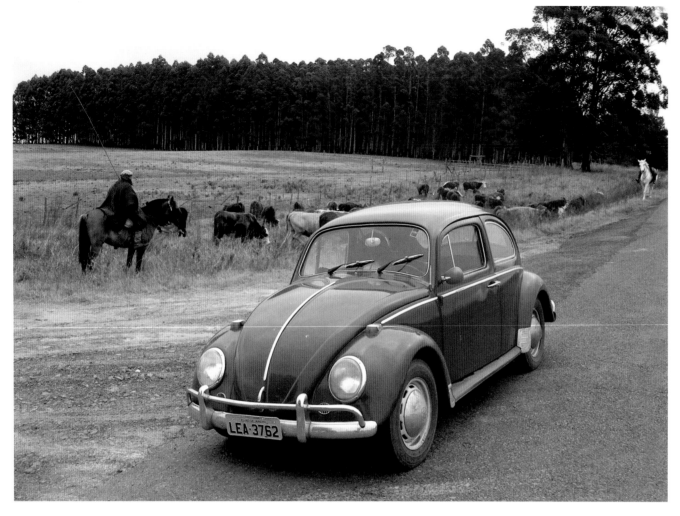

of the Beetle, although other models continued to be built. The last Beetle (or so it seemed at the time) left Sao Paulo on 7 December 1986, making a grand total of 3,300,000 built between 1959 and 1986. During this time, the Fusca had developed from a basic 1200cc model to a 1600cc, dual-carburettor, alcohol-fuelled saloon with disc brakes and rear stabilizer bar. This, perhaps, is the sort of model which Volkswagen in Germany should have built instead of the less-than-successful 1302 and 1303 models, but then hindsight is always perfect.

Ironically, one of the reasons behind the Beetle's demise in Brazil – the increasing affluence of the people – was partly responsible for its amazing reintroduction some eight years later. The government, led now by President Itamar Franco, became acutely aware that there was a large sector of the population which, although unable to afford an expensive car, was in a position to buy a basic vehicle, should one be available. With the loss of the Beetle from the Volkswagen range, there was no suitable low-cost model. Similarly, more affluent families, who wished to own a second or third car, were unable to buy the Beetles they wanted. There was also the small matter of inexpensive Japanese imported cars swamping the country,

SP-2 and the highly successful Brasilia hatchback before being replaced himself in July 1973 by Wolfgang Sauer. Sauer was credited with consolidating Volkswagen's domination of the domestic market at the same time as increasing the company's share of export sales.

In 1972, a total of 223,453 locally manufactured Beetles were sold – that's an average of some 18,600 per month – which accounted for

almost half of all vehicles sold on the Brazilian market. A further 6,000 Fuscas were also exported and, by March 1972, the total production of the model reached the 1,000,000 mark. Two years later, sales had climbed to 237,323, of which 24,474 were sent abroad, while June 1976 saw the 2,000,000th Brazilian Beetle leave the assembly line. There appeared to be no stopping the success of the Fusca, with exports

reaching no fewer than 60 countries around the world.

Falling Demand

However, demand for the Beetle, by whatever name, began to fall slowly as the nation became more affluent and Brazilians began to buy better-equipped cars. With sales dropping to just 34,000 units in 1984, the decision was made to halt production to the detriment of the economy. According to Rainer Wolf, executive manager in charge of Volkswagen's South American marketing division, market research showed that the new owner was most likely to be a male, 40+ years of age and married; he would be conservative in his tastes and have an eye for value for money.

A New Beginning

On 4 February 1993, following pressure from President Franco, the Brazilian government signed a document, called a Protocol Of Intent, allowing the state-funded car industry, Autolatina, to back the reintroduction of the Fusca to the tune of some $30,000,000. This led to the creation of 800 new jobs at Sao Paulo, in addition to a further 24,000 as part of the massive infrastructure necessary to market and service the new cars. It was estimated that a total of 100,000 people would directly benefit from this programme. A production target of 24,000 cars per year was set, with the reborn Beetle selling for the equivalent at the time of £7,200; this figure included 0.1 per cent Industrial Products Tax, 2 per cent manufacturer's social security contribution and a corresponding 2 per cent dealer contribution.

There was good reasoning behind the decision to reintroduce the Beetle, as opposed to designing an entirely new model, aside from the most obvious advantage of

not having to manufacture new press tooling. For, despite Brazil's increasing affluence, the road system was still in a poor state and, of the estimated 1,500,000km (93,200 miles) of highways, only 9 per cent were paved. This meant that for those people living outside the major conurbations, any car had to be capable of standing up to use in rugged conditions. With the exception of four-wheel-drive vehicles, the Beetle was the only car suited to the terrain.

The Final Chapter?

The new Beetle was assembled in an 8,000m² (86,000sq ft) wing of the Anchieta Industrial Unit at Sao Bernardo do Campo in Sao Paulo. The building housed a new, fully-automated, production line which was a far cry from the original rented shed, where the CKD models were assembled at the very beginning of Beetle assembly in Brazil some 40 years earlier. The first completed car rolled off the line on 23 August 1993.

Even then, it was clearly a strong possibility that the Brazilian Beetle would represent the final chapter in the development of the People's Car as we knew it and, as such, it is worth taking a detailed look at its specification. Based very much on the European models of the early 1970s, the Fusca was a flat-screen Beetle equipped with torsion-bar front suspension and swing-axle rear. It was powered by a 1584cc engine, with

dual Solex H32PDSIT carburettors and had a compression ratio of 10.0:1 to allow it to burn domestically-produced, wood-based, alcohol fuel. The result was a power output of 58.7bhp (SAE) produced at 4,300rpm, with maximum torque of 11.9kg m (86lb ft) at just 2,800rpm. In line with the then-current emission laws, the exhaust system was fitted with a catalytic converter located under the rear valance, with the main silencer being tucked up under the driver's-side rear wing. A single tailpipe exited under the wheel arch. The transmission was a special "sealed for life" version of the traditional four-speed manual transaxle fitted to the majority of Beetles since 1962. The dual-circuit braking system consisted of disc brakes on the front, with drums at the rear.

As far as interior trim was concerned, the re-born Fusca came with a plastic padded dashboard (simply a cover fitted over the old pressed steel panel) into which was set a square speedometer, calibrated to 160km/h (100mph), the design of which seemed at odds with the car's rather old-fashioned styling. To the right of this was a fuel gauge, while to the left was space for an optional clock. The steering wheel was moulded from deformable black plastic, and looked similar to those fitted to most Volkswagens in the 1970s. In the centre of the horn push was a Volkswagen roundel logo. The seats were far better than anything previously offered in a basic Beetle, being trimmed in velour material

with separate head restraints, reinforced frames and mountings and a reclining mechanism. Redesigned seat belt anchorage points, front and back, further helped to improve passenger safety.

The factory claimed a 0–100km/h (0–62mph) time of just 14.5 seconds, with a maximum speed of 140km/h (87mph). The fuel economy was not ground-breaking by any means, with an average consumption of just 9km/l (approximately 25mpg), although it has to be remembered that this figure was achieved using extremely cheap alcohol-based fuel. It is interesting to note that the coefficient of drag (Cd) was stated as being 0.48, somewhat worse than the 0.44 figure claimed by Wolfsburg for its Beetle in the 1970s.

The new Fusca was launched in a range of three standard colours – Star White, Arena Beige and Saturn Blue – along with five optional colours: Universal Black, Sports Red, Lunar Silver, Athenas Beige Metallic and Pine Green Metallic. In addition, two option packages were offered from the very beginning. Package 1 consisted of a clock, foam-covered sports steering wheel, dual horns, door pockets, a carpeted strip on the bottom of the door panels, protective rubber strips on the bumpers and a passenger-side door mirror. Package 2 added a heated rear windscreen, green-tinted windows, opening rear-side windows, tinted rear light lenses and a digital stereo system.

This, then, was how the Beetle would find yet another new lease of life in the 1990s in South America – in many ways a far cry from the original, no-nonsense People's Car of the late 1930s, and yet, in other ways, so similar. After all, was it not the word of Germany's then leader that led to the introduction of a cheap car for the masses, in the same way that, in 1993, the Brazilian President pushed for Volkswagen to reintroduce the Beetle to provide that same inexpensive transport for his people? And, remarkably, in a marketplace now bursting at the seams with more modern alternatives, that would give the Beetle yet another bite of the cherry in Brazil, that this time lasted until 1996.

Full Circle

So, for a little while longer, the Beetle would live on, and the words of a somewhat confused official press release, issued on the reintroduction of the Fusca, could almost have been those of a political speech made 60 years earlier in a restless Germany: *"As a popular car, it fits into the brand's renewal programme, which heads an industrial policy that aims at the production of cars for all the social segments. In terms of its characteristics and cost-benefit advantages already experienced by the consumers, the Fusca will conquer its rightful niche within the market, a niche in which rationality and attributes that are considerably differentiated in relation to other models in the same line,*

predominate. Volkswagen's Marketing Planning Division envisages that the Fusca will win a 10 per cent market share to begin with in the popular car segment, the average demand of which is estimated at between 20,000 and 25,000 units per year."

In the end, though, it was Mexico that had the final, final word in the long production history of the classic Beetle. When Brazilian production stopped again, in 1996 so far as the true classic Beetle was concerned, it stopped for good – but Mexico still wasn't quite done yet, as the Beetle, almost unbelievably, clung on towards the 21st century.

Unsurprisingly, perhaps, Mexico offered little more than token changes during the twilight years of the car's production life: exterior trim was simplified, ventilation was improved, at opposite ends of the scale new budget versions and new up-spec versions were offered, but all the time the production figures continued to click up – although clearly now at a far more modest rate than in the Beetle's heyday. By 1998 they were exclusively for domestic sale; and while the biggest single role for the Beetle in Mexico had long been as a green-and-white-liveried official taxi, even that was compromised (if not actually ended) by a new government decree that all taxis henceforth had to have four doors – which no production Beetle ever had.

The final milestone on Mexico's watch was probably inevitable. By

2003, production was down to around 30,000 cars a year, against a peak of 1.3 million in 1971 – leaving the all-time target's fall as just a matter of time. It came in 1997, when the Toyota Corolla finally displaced the Beetle at the top of the all-time biggest-selling passenger car chart, where it had survived for some 25 years after overtaking the Ford Model T in 1972. Again, whether the eighth generation front-drive Corolla that took the record had as much in common with the first 1966 rear-drive Corolla as a 1997 Beetle did with a 1948 Type 1 Saloon is debatable, but the Corolla nameplate, not the Beetle was now the world's biggest seller. By 2015, in its eleventh generation, the Corolla was close to doubling total Beetle production, while Volkswagen's own Golf had also comfortably passed the 30,000,000 mark.

The final Beetle total was 21,529,464 cars, the last of which came off the Mexican assembly line, with appropriate ceremony, on 30 July 2003, immediately to be despatched to pride of place alongside so many other historic Beetles in the Volkswagen museum.

After "normal" production ended on 10 July, the final flourish was the run of 3,000 special edition cars designated Sedan Ultima Edicion, and selling at a premium, at around 84,000 Pesos, where the final standard model had listed at 68,000. The Final Editions came in either Aquarius Blue (as the very last) or Harvest Moon beige, with chrome

trim, body-coloured wheel rims and whitewall tyres. The final car was nicknamed El Rey, The King.

In 1994, at the Detroit Motor Show, Volkswagen showed a concept car called simply "Concept 1", styled by Freeman Thomas and J Mays at Volkswagen and Audi's American Design Center in California. It unmistakably evoked the classic Beetle, as the New MINI evoked the classic Mini, but in the New Beetle's case, in shape alone, as below the skin it would be front-engined, front-drive, and essentially wholly conventional. It evolved with a cabriolet version at the 1995 Geneva Show, and was so well received that the outcome was obvious. By 1996 it was officially referred to as the New Beetle, and that's how it was launched into production in 1997 – to be assembled in the Puebla plant in Mexico.

It was well received, and in broad terms it was a commercial success, but the New Beetle was not a new Beetle. The original was not so easily replaced as that.●

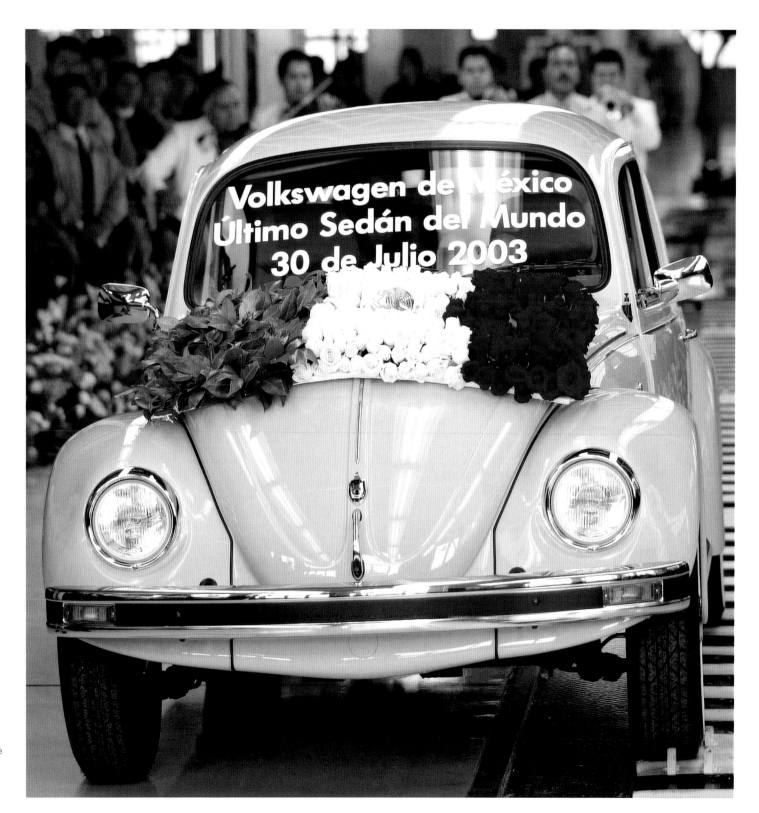

Right 65 years after its launch, and after 58 years of production, the last Beetle, number 21,529,464, rolled off the production line in Puebla, Mexico on 30 July 2003.

the cars

Compare the 1938 VW38 Saloon with the
1990 Mexican Type 1, and it is clear that the
story of the Beetle is a story of continuous
evolution while following a single clearly defined
bloodline. Perhaps more than any other car in
the world, where the same badge might have
survived through several fundamentally different
generations, the core elements of the Beetle remain
instantly recognizable through its entire lifespan,
in saloon or cabriolet variants, and even the
occasional branch off the main family tree, from
Kübelwagen to Karmann Ghia, Schwimmwagen
to Stoll Coupé and Type 2 Combi. It is one
more thing that makes the Beetle special, and
the evolution began virtually from Day One.

NSU Type 32 Prototype

Following his first attempts at building a Volksauto, or People's Car, in association with the Zündapp motorcycle company, Ferdinand Porsche embarked on a new project with Fritz von Falkenhayn of the successful NSU organization. The result, in 1934, of this collaboration was Project No 32: an aerodynamic saloon powered by an air-cooled, horizontally-opposed four-cylinder engine. The chosen suspension medium was Porsche's beloved torsion bar. A total of three examples were built, of which just one survives in the AutoMuseum at Wolfsburg. This is the oldest surviving vehicle which can be considered a true Volkswagen prototype.

Right In this profile view of the sole-surviving NSU prototype, it is possible to make out the familiar lines of the Beetle. From the very beginning, Porsche preferred the idea of an aerodynamic, rear-engined vehicle to the more traditional upright designs of the period.

1934

Left   A number of headlamp configurations were tried. The units shown here are not the originals.

Top left   Unlike the production models of the future, the windscreen wipers of the 1932 prototype were located at the top of the windscreen and swept outwards. The oval-shaped interior mirror is similar to those fitted to the first Beetles.

Top right   The vents behind the rear side windows were to allow air to the engine. This is one feature which did not make it into production.

Above The dashboard was unique to the model, featuring an octagonal speedometer and scattered minor controls. The emergency (hand) brake was situated beneath the dashboard and can be seen below the speedometer.

Left The engine was a horizontally-opposed, air-cooled flat four, like that of the Beetle, but with a capacity of 1467cc. The power output was a modest 28bhp, which allowed the Type 32 to reach a maximum speed of 90km/h (56mph).

ENGINE

Horizontally opposed, air-cooled four cylinder.

Construction: Two-piece cast alloy crankcase split vertically with separate cast-iron cylinders and cast aluminium-alloy pistons. Four main bearings. Cast aluminium cylinder heads with individual inlet ports.

Bore and stroke: 80mm x 73mm.

Capacity: 1467cc (89.5ci).

Valves: Pushrod operated overhead.

Compression ratio: n/a.

Fuel system: Mechanical fuel pump; single Solex carburettor.

Maximum power: 28bhp (32 US hp) at 3,300rpm.

Maximum torque: n/a.

TRANSMISSION

Four-speed manual, non-synchromesh transaxle with integral final drive unit. Two-piece casing.

Gear ratios: n/a.

BRAKES

Cable-operated drums on all four wheels.

STEERING

Worm and nut.

SUSPENSION

Front: Fully independent with transverse torsion bars and telescopic shock absorbers. King- and link-pin design.

Rear: Fully independent swing-axle with twin torsion bars and lever arm shock absorbers.

WHEELS AND TYRES

4J x 16in pressed steel wheels. 5.20 x 16 cross-ply tyres.

DIMENSIONS

Length: n/a.

Width: n/a.

Height: n/a.

Wheelbase: 2400mm (7ft 10.5in).

Dry weight: 790kg (1742lb).

PERFORMANCE

Maximum speed: 90km/h (55mph).

Acceleration: 0–96km/h (60mph): n/a.

Fuel consumption: n/a.

NUMBER BUILT

(1934) 3

1938

VW38 Saloon

By the end of the 1930s, Porsche was at last able to prove to himself that the concept of a People's Car was a sound one. Following extensive testing of the prototype VW38 cars, of which a series of 44 was built, the full go-ahead was given for the production of the KdF-Wagen. Unfortunately, the onset of war effectively brought the KdF project to a halt, at least as far as the general public was concerned. This VW38, which bears the chassis number 3803, is the last survivor of the original pre-production prototypes and can be seen in the Auto-Museum at Wolfsburg. At last, the familiar Beetle shape had been established. It was indeed the beginning of a legend.

Left The familiar lines were finalized with the last of the pre-war prototypes. Note the absence of any superfluous adornment – this was a vehicle being built down to what Porsche believed was an unrealistically low price. Every saving helped.

Right The rear of the VW38 has a slightly more rounded style than later production models, but is essentially the same. Note the air-intake louvres under the rear windows. The front view shows the single externally-mounted horn, the simple blade bumpers and the so-called "banana" curved over-riders.

1938

Left It is not difficult to see why these were frequently referred to as "banana" over-riders. This design was finally superseded in 1949.

Top far right The small oval-shaped mirror was similar to that used on the first production models, as was the three-point fixing.

Above left Trim remained simple, with plain door panels being uncluttered except for the functional handles to operate the windows and open the doors.

Above centre The interior light was located above and between the two split rear windows. Note the lack of headlining around the glass, which did little to help reduce noise levels inside the vehicle.

Above right The position of the emergency (hand) brake had moved from below the dashboard to between the front seats.

Above The dashboard layout of the VW38 was simple but attractive, with two open glove boxes and a pair of central panels, one of which housed the speedometer – the second panel displayed a diagram of the gearshift pattern. This dashboard layout would remain fundamentally unchanged until 1953.

Left The engine produced 24bhp from its 985cc at a lowly 3,000rpm. This allowed the vehicle to reach a maximum cruising speed of 97km/h (60mph). The unit proved to be extremely reliable and saw service for a further eight years.

ENGINE

Horizontally opposed, air-cooled four cylinder.

Construction: Two-piece cast magnesium-alloy crankcase split vertically with separate cast-iron cylinders and cast aluminium-alloy pistons. Four main bearings. Cast aluminium cylinder heads with siamesed inlet ports.

Bore and stroke: 70mm x 64mm.

Capacity: 985cc (42ci).

Valves: Pushrod operated overhead.

Compression ratio: n/a.

Fuel system: Mechanical fuel pump; single Solex carburettor.

Maximum power: 24bhp (30 US hp) at 3,000rpm.

Maximum torque: n/a.

TRANSMISSION

Four-speed manual, non-synchromesh transaxle with integral final drive unit. Two-piece casing.

Gear ratios: First - 3.60; second - 2.07; third - 1.25; fourth - 0.80; reverse - 6.60.

Final drive ratio: 4.43:1.

BRAKES

Cable-operated drums on all four wheels.

STEERING

Worm and nut.

SUSPENSION

Front: Fully independent with transverse, multi-leaf torsion bars and telescopic shock absorbers. King- and link-pin design.

Rear: Fully independent swing-axle with twin solid torsion bars and lever arm shock absorbers.

WHEELS AND TYRES

4J x 16in pressed steel wheels. 4.25 x 16 cross-ply tyres.

DIMENSIONS

Length: 4070mm (13ft 4.2in).

Width: 1540mm (5ft 0.6in).

Height: 1500mm (4ft 11in).

Wheelbase: 2400mm (7ft 10.5in).

Dry weight: 780kg (1720lb).

PERFORMANCE

Maximum speed: 97km/h (60mph).

Acceleration: 0–96km/h (60mph): n/a.

Fuel consumption: n/a.

NUMBER BUILT

(1938) 44

1938

VW38 Cabriolet

From the very beginning, a cabriolet version of the People's Car had been envisaged. Indeed, the early "V" series of prototypes, built in 1935, had included a cabriolet, designated the V2. The example shown is the earliest survivor and carries the chassis number 31. Soundly constructed, the VW38 cabriolet shared the same chassis and running gear as the contemporary saloon model and proved to be very popular among the high-ranking officialdom of the time. Several photographs exist of Adolf Hitler and Hermann Goering showing great interest in the VW38 cabriolet, and Hitler rode in one at the factory cornerstone-laying ceremony in May 1938.

Right The overall styling of the VW38 cabriolet prototype was very elegant, especially with the well-made hood folded down. This sole-surviving example now resides in the AutoMuseum at Wolfsburg.

Right From the front, the revised shape of the windscreen surround is evident. The flatter shape was adopted for greater strength. At the rear, note the air-intake louvres are still in the main bodywork below the rear window. Post-war models would have them punched into the engine lid where they proved more efficient when the roof was folded down.

Left The semaphore turn signals were mounted externally. On the first post-war production versions, they were mounted in the quarter-panel itself.

Right The doors differed from those of the saloon in that there was no fixed window surround. Instead, the frame rose and fell with the window itself.

Far right Wedges in the rear edge of the doors prevented flexing, by locating in cut-outs in the door pillar.

Left   The emergency (hand) brake is located between the front seats and actuates all four drum brakes by way of a rod linkage. Ahead of the brake lever can be seen the gear lever.

Above   So that the driver could see over the top of the hood when it was folded down, the driving mirror was designed to hinge up or down. It is shown here in the lower position.

Right   The dashboard of the cabriolet was essentially the same as that of the saloon. The white switch at the top of the dashboard operates the turn signals.

Left Mechanically, the 1938 cabriolet was identical to its saloon stablemate, with a 985cc engine and non-synchromesh, four-speed transmission. Note the simple "mushroom" air-filter fitted to the tiny Solex carburettor. The cooling fan and generator were driven from the crankshaft by a single belt. If this broke, the engine would quickly overheat and soon seize.

ENGINE

Horizontally opposed, air-cooled four cylinder.

Construction: Two-piece cast magnesium-alloy crankcase split vertically with separate cast-iron cylinders and cast aluminium-alloy pistons. Four main bearings. Cast aluminium cylinder heads with siamesed inlet ports.

Bore and stroke: 70mm x 64mm.

Capacity: 985cc (42ci).

Valves: Pushrod operated overhead.

Compression ratio: n/a.

Fuel system: Mechanical fuel pump; single Solex carburettor.

Maximum power: 24bhp (30 US hp) at 3,000rpm.

Maximum torque: n/a.

TRANSMISSION

Four-speed manual, non-synchromesh transaxle with integral final drive unit. Two-piece casing.

Gear ratios: First - 3.60; second - 2.07; third - 1.25; fourth - 0.80; reverse - 6.60.

Final drive ratio: 4.43:1.

BRAKES

Cable-operated drums on all four wheels.

STEERING

Worm and nut.

SUSPENSION

Front: Fully independent with transverse, multi-leaf torsion bars and telescopic shock absorbers. King- and link-pin design.

Rear: Fully independent swing-axle with twin solid torsion bars and lever arm shock absorbers.

WHEELS AND TYRES

4J x 16in pressed steel wheels. 4.25 x 16 cross-ply tyres.

DIMENSIONS

Length: 4070mm (13ft 4.2in).

Width: 1540mm (5ft 0.6in).

Height: 1500mm (4ft 11in).

Wheelbase: 2400mm (7ft 10.5in).

Dry weight: 780kg (1720lb).

PERFORMANCE

Maximum speed: 97km/h (60mph).

Acceleration: 0–96km/h (60mph): n/a.

Fuel consumption: n/a.

NUMBER BUILT

(1938) n/a.

Type 82 Kübelwagen

The Type 82 Kübelwagen remains the best-known of all wartime derivations of the KdF-Wagen. The simple, but rugged, Jeep-like vehicle saw extensive use throughout World War II. Although only supplied with two-wheel drive, the Type 82 was a most accomplished off-road vehicle. Due to its light weight, the Kübelwagen proved to be particularly well-suited for use on both the Russian Front – where thick, glutinous mud proved to be the downfall of heavier machines – and the North African desert, where it was able to cope with soft sand. Reliable and easy to maintain, the Type 82 was one of the most successful military vehicles ever made.

Left The Kübelwagen was one of the most successful military vehicles used by the Wehrmacht. The simple, slab-sided body was produced by Ambi-Budd in Berlin. Note the sharply sloping nose, which allowed the driver to view the road ahead more easily, the front-mounted spare wheel and the crude weather protection.

Right Most drivers preferred to run with the hood down as the improved visibility made driving easier. The engine was protected from damage by a substantial skid-plate. Two tow hooks were provided to allow easy recovery.

Left The hood offered minimal protection against the elements, especially the cold of the Russian Front. However, something was better than nothing. Note the air-intake louvres under the rear window area and the large engine cover.

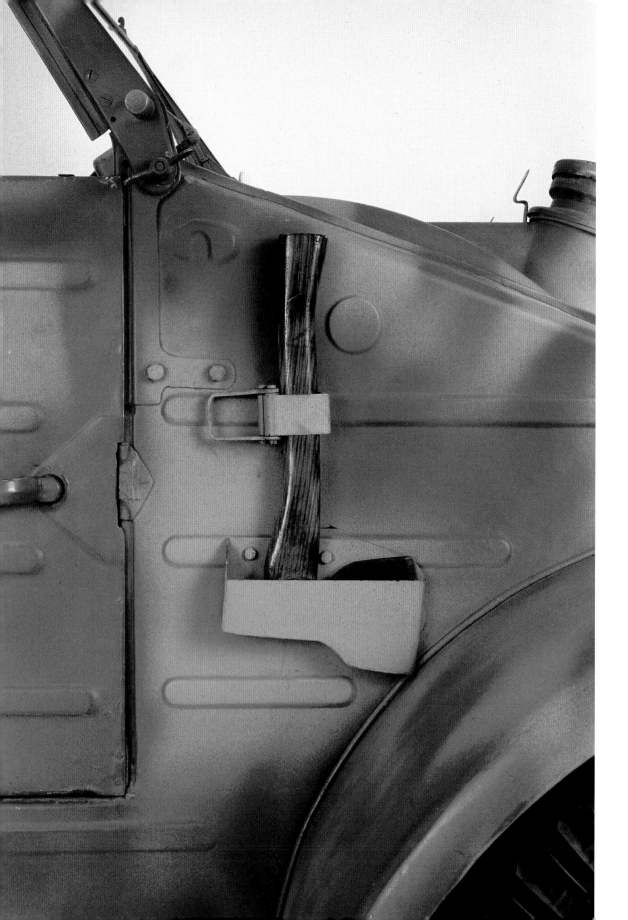

Left and top left Most Kübelwagens were equipped with tools of some kind to help the occupants dig themselves out of an awkward situation. An axe and a shovel were typically fitted.

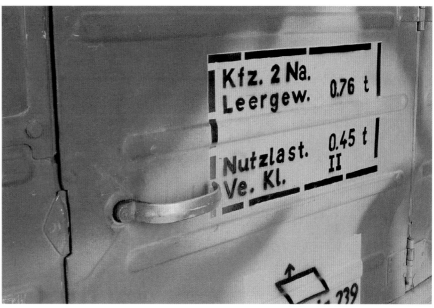

Kfz. 2 Na.
Leergew. 0.76 t

Nutzlast. 0.45 t
Ve. Kl. II

Top left   When conditions allowed, the windscreen could be folded flat, giving the driver a better view. This feature also allowed the vehicle to be more easily transported on a train or larger truck. The Type 82 was the epitome of function over form, with nothing fitted which did not have a purpose.

Bottom left   The dashboard layout was quite unlike that of any previous vehicle. In the centre is the speedometer and switch gear, while to the left is a small stowage area. Either side of the speedometer is a pair of fuse boxes, while at the base of the folding windscreen are two windscreen wiper motors. Note the grab rail.

Far right   In common with all other KdF models, the emergency (hand) brake was located between the front seats. Note the wooden duckboards on the floor ahead of the seating.

Left The engine for the early Kübelwagens was the original 24bhp, 985cc unit but this example, having been built in 1944, uses the more powerful 1131cc engine. Engine access is very good. Note the air-filter.

ENGINE

Horizontally opposed, air-cooled four cylinder.

Construction: Two-piece cast magnesium-alloy crankcase split vertically with separate cast-iron cylinders and cast aluminium-alloy pistons. Four main bearings. Cast aluminium cylinder heads with siamesed inlet ports.

Bore and stroke: 75mm x 64mm.

Capacity: 1131cc (69ci).

Valves: Pushrod operated overhead.

Compression ratio: n/a.

Fuel system: Mechanical fuel pump; single Solex carburettor.

Maximum power: 25bhp (31 US hp) at 3,000rpm.

Maximum torque: 7.60mkg at 2,000rpm.

TRANSMISSION

Four-speed manual, non-syncromesh transaxle with integral final drive unit. Limited slip differential. Two-piece casing.

Gear ratios: First - 3.60; second - 2.07; third - 1.25; fourth - 0.80; reverse - 6.60.

Final drive ratio: 4.43:1.

Reduction gear ratio: 1.4:1.

BRAKES

Cable-operated drums on all four wheels.

STEERING

Worm and nut.

SUSPENSION

Front: Fully independent with transverse, multi-leaf torsion bars and telescopic shock absorbers. King- and link-pin design.

Rear: Fully independent swing-axle with twin solid torsion bars and lever arm shock absorbers. Reduction gear on rear axles.

WHEELS AND TYRES

4J x 16in pressed steel wheels. 5.25 x 16 cross-ply tyres.

DIMENSIONS

Length: 3740mm (12ft 3.2in).

Width: 1600mm (5ft 3in).

Height: Top raised 1650mm (5ft 5in); Top lowered 1111mm (3ft 7.7in).

Wheelbase: 2400mm (7ft 10.5in).

Dry weight: 725kg (1598lb).

PERFORMANCE

Maximum speed: 80km/h (50mph).

Acceleration: 0–96km/h (60mph): n/a.

Fuel consumption: 8lts/100km (30mpg).

NUMBER BUILT

(1940–1945) 50,000

1944

Type 166 Schwimmwagen

When the Waffen SS approached Porsche about the possibility of fitting a KdF-Wagen engine into a motorcycle, so as to produce a compact go-anywhere machine, the discussions led to the design and development of the Type 166. This fascinating amphibious vehicle had a wheelbase some 400mm (15.75in) less than that of the Kübelwagen and enjoyed the benefits of all-wheel drive. Powered by the same air-cooled four-cylinder engine as its stablemate, the Type 166 was fitted with a propeller driven from the end of the crankshaft to provide propulsion in water. This is regarded as one of the most versatile military vehicles ever built.

Left   This rear three-quarter view gives a good indication of the boat-like nature of the Schwimmwagen. Note the high-mounted exhaust system and the crude air-intake grille behind the cockpit.

Right The tub-like shape of the Schwimmwagen can be clearly seen in these views. The large engine access panel was designed to help prevent water from getting into the engine bay – the high sides being well above the water line.

Top right When the Schwimmwagen was in water, it was commonplace to fold the windscreen down. This also facilitated transportation. A cover was provided to protect the windscreen when not in use. Note the single windscreen wiper motor and the front-mounted spare wheel. The fuel filler cap is just ahead of the windscreen.

Bottom right Drive to the front wheels was achieved via these drive shafts which were located just behind the familiar king- and link-pin suspension set-up.

Above The simple hood folded down out of the way but offered little protection when raised. Rudimentary mudguards offered similarly minimal protection.

Above left With the retaining strap released, the propeller could be swung down into position. It engaged with a drive shaft which exited the bodywork in line with the crankshaft. The substantial guard around the propeller was to protect it from damage in shallow waters – and almost certainly helped to keep fingers and toes out of harm's way!

Above right The propeller could be raised to allow the vehicle to be used on the road. This was achieved by hinging it up out of the way using a tool supplied with each Schwimmwagen. The propeller was then secured to the bodywork with a leather strap.

Above The dashboard of the Type 166 was even more rudimentary than that of the Kübelwagen. The central switch panel housed a tiny speedometer and other minor controls. In front of the driver were the instructions for selecting four-wheel drive and use of the special low-ratio gear. A simple black three-spoke steering wheel was identical to that of the Kübel. Control levers between the seats included the gear lever and the selector for high and low ratios, and four-wheel drive. The extra pedal on the floor operated an automatic greasing facility.

Left The engine is also the later 1131cc unit but is equipped with an air-filter which draws air from above the vehicle to prevent the ingress of water. The engine is used in conjunction with a four-speed transmission which features a limited-slip differential and power take-off for the front wheels. The four-wheel-drive system was developed for the Schwimmwagen but later saw limited use on some Type 877 saloons. The drive for the propeller was taken from the end of the crankshaft. The engine bay was efficiently sealed to keep water out.

ENGINE

Horizontally opposed, air-cooled four cylinder.
Construction: Two-piece cast magnesium-alloy crankcase split vertically with separate cast-iron cylinders and cast aluminium-alloy pistons. Four main bearings. Cast aluminium cylinder heads with siamesed inlet ports.
Bore and stroke: 75mm x 64mm.
Capacity: 1131cc (69ci).
Valves: Pushrod operated overhead.
Compression ratio: 5.8:1.
Fuel system: Mechanical fuel pump; single Solex carburettor.
Maximum power: 25bhp (31 US hp) at 3,000rpm.
Maximum torque: 7.60mkg at 2,000rpm.

TRANSMISSION

Four-wheel drive with four-speed manual, non-synchromesh transaxle with integral final drive unit. Limited slip differential. Two-piece casing.
Gear ratios: First - 3.60; second - 2.07; third - 1.25; fourth - 0.80; reverse - 6.60.
Final drive ratio: 4.43:1.
Reduction gear ratio: 1.4:1. Propeller driven from crankshaft.

BRAKES

Cable-operated drums on all four wheels.

STEERING

Worm and nut.

SUSPENSION

Front: Fully independent with transverse, multi-leaf torsion bars and telescopic shock absorbers. King- and link-pin design.
Rear: Fully independent swing-axle with twin solid torsion bars and lever arm shock absorbers. Reduction gears on rear axles.

WHEELS AND TYRES

4J x 16in pressed steel wheels. 5.20 x 16 cross-ply tyres.

DIMENSIONS

Length: 3825mm (12ft 6.6in).
Width: 1480mm (4ft 10.3in).
Height: 1615mm (5ft 3.6in).
Wheelbase: 2000mm (6ft 6.7in).
Dry weight: 890kg (1962lb).

PERFORMANCE

Maximum speed: on land 80km/h (50mph); on water 10km/h (6mph).
Acceleration: 0–96km/h (60mph): n/a.
Fuel consumption: n/a.

NUMBER BUILT

(1942–1944) 14,283

Type 82E

With the prospect of a war looming large on the horizon, Porsche was forced to turn his attentions towards developing military versions of the KdF-Wagen, one such example being the Type 82E. This vehicle featured the regular saloon body mounted on the high-riding running gear of the Type 82 Kübelwagen. The resultant increase in ground clearance greatly improved its off-road capabilities, thereby rendering it suitable for use by the Wehrmacht in all theatres of war. In 1941, a four-wheel-drive version, the Type 877 or Kommandeurwagen, was developed from the Type 82E, although only a relatively small number of these were built.

Left   The high-riding stance of the Type 82E is due to the adoption of the reduction-type rear axle and front spindle assemblies fitted to the Type 82 Kübelwagen.

Right From the front, it is easy to
appreciate the increased ride height.
The idea behind this was to give the
Type 82E better off-road capabilities.
Note the total lack of embellishment
– after all, this was intended to be a
serious military vehicle. The simple
blade bumpers and over-riders are
similar to those fitted to the VW38.

Left From the rear, the 1943 military Type 82E looks very little different to the earlier 1938 VW38 prototypes. Note the single exhaust tail pipe which exits centrally under the rear valance.

Top left   KdF-model Beetles were all fitted with this round fuel tank. The bracket in front of it is for carrying the spare wheel. Note the substantial front bulkhead design and exposed front suspension.

Bottom left   The dashboard layout is virtually identical to that of the last of the pre-war prototypes, with its two open glove boxes and a single gauge panel housing the speedometer. Note the blanking plate which now has the famous KdF "cogwheel" logo stamped into it. The steering wheel is the same as that of earlier models.

Top right   In the absence of a fuel gauge, a three-position (on-off-reserve) fuel tap was fitted. This could be operated, at a stretch, by the driver's foot. It is shown here in the "on" position.

Top far right   The chassis plate, to the left of the fuel tank, shows year of manufacture, weight and model type.

Bottom far right   The running boards of the Type 82E differed from the later versions by having these metal end caps fitted over the top of the rubber moulding.

Above The semaphore turn signals are mounted externally in metal boxes located at the base of each windscreen pillar.

Left The 1131cc engine was first introduced early in 1943 and produced 25bhp at 3,300rpm. This was only just sufficient to meet the minimum requirements laid down by the German military authorities. Note the air-filter designed to cope with desert conditions.

ENGINE

Horizontally opposed, air-cooled four cylinder.

Construction: Two-piece cast magnesium-alloy crankcase split vertically with separate cast-iron cylinders and cast aluminium-alloy pistons. Four main bearings. Cast aluminium cylinder heads with siamesed inlet ports.

Bore and stroke: 75mm x 64mm.

Capacity: 1131cc (69ci).

Valves: Pushrod operated overhead.

Compression ratio: 5.8:1.

Fuel system: Mechanical fuel pump; single Solex 26VFJ carburettor.

Maximum power: 25bhp (31 US hp) at 3,300rpm.

Maximum torque: 49lb ft at 2,000rpm.

TRANSMISSION

Four-speed manual, non-synchromesh transaxle with integral final drive unit. Two-piece casing.

Gear ratios: First - 3.60; second - 2.07; third - 1.25; fourth - 0.80; reverse - 6.60.

Final drive ratio: 4.43:1.

Reduction gear ratio: 1.4:1.

BRAKES

Cable-operated drums on all four wheels.

STEERING

Worm and nut.

SUSPENSION

Front: Fully independent with transverse, multi-leaf torsion bars and telescopic shock absorbers. King- and link-pin design.

Rear: Fully independent swing-axle with twin solid torsion bars and lever arm shock absorbers. Reduction gears on rear axles.

WHEELS AND TYRES

4J x 16in pressed steel wheels. 5.20 x 16 cross-ply tyres.

DIMENSIONS

Length: 4070mm (13ft 4.2in).

Width: 1540mm (5ft 0.6in).

Height: 1600mm (5ft 3in).

Wheelbase: 2400mm (7ft 10.5in).

Dry weight: 780kg (1720lb).

PERFORMANCE

Maximum speed: 80km/h (50mph).

Acceleration: 0–96km/h (60mph): n/a.

Fuel consumption: n/a.

NUMBER BUILT

(1942–1944) 546

1948
Type 1 Saloon

When the British Army appointed Heinz Nordhoff the
General Director of Volkswagen in January 1948, the factory
was producing some 2,500 cars per month. The vehicles,
however, were little more than upgraded versions of the old
pre-war prototypes, equipped with the 1131cc engine of the
Schwimmwagen. Volkswagens of this era, as typified by the
example shown here, were basic in the extreme, without
chrome trim or any other non-functional adornment. However,
Nordhoff realized that, for the Volkswagen saloon to appeal
to a wider market, changes would have to be made and the
following year, a special export model was introduced.

Right A lack of chrome trim was a reflection not only of a cost-cutting mentality, but also of the shortage of raw materials at the time. Note the single, angled exhaust pipe and the location of the rear lights low down on each rear wing. From the front, little has changed since the days of the wartime Type 82E.

Bottom left The design of the exterior door handle was little changed – opening the door was simply a matter of pulling the handle. Only the driver-side locked from outside.

Top right The shape of the interior light had now been finalized as a round design.

Bottom right The semaphore turn signals were now located in the door pillars, where they would remain until their demise in the late 1950s.

Above The dashboard layout differed little from that of the VW38 prototypes. The right-hand blanking panel featured the familiar VW logo. All visual references to the old KdF movement had now disappeared. The speedometer design changed little.

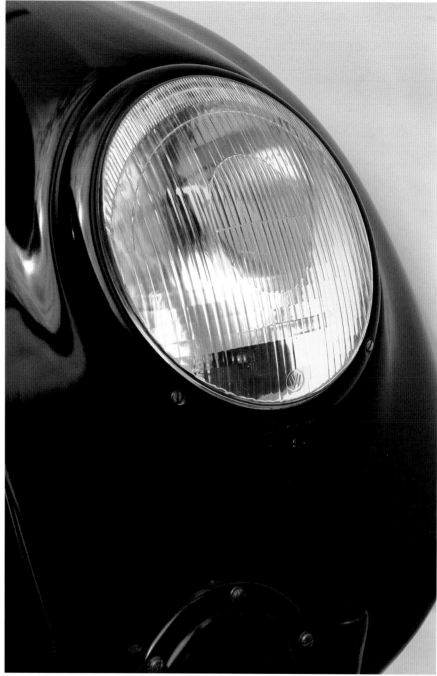

Above left   The so-called "Pope's Nose" number-plate light also incorporated the brake warning light. On early vehicles, the number plate was mounted on a raised pressing in the engine lid.

Above right The luggage space could be accessed by turning this "L" handle which was similar to that fitted at the rear of the vehicle.

Left The engine cooling shroud is clearly marked with instructions on how to set the internal flaps for use in summer or winter. The 1131cc engine produced 25bhp and was essentially the same as that fitted to the earlier military models.

ENGINE

Horizontally opposed, air-cooled four cylinder.

Construction: Two-piece cast magnesium-alloy crankcase split vertically with separate cast-iron cylinders and cast aluminium-alloy pistons. Four main bearings. Cast aluminium cylinder heads with siamesed inlet ports.

Bore and stroke: 75mm x 64mm.

Capacity: 1131cc (69ci).

Valves: Pushrod operated overhead.

Compression ratio: 5.8:1.

Fuel system: Mechanical fuel pump; single Solex 26VFI carburettor.

Maximum power: 25bhp (31 US hp) at 3,300rpm.

Maximum torque: 49lb ft at 2,000rpm.

TRANSMISSION

Four-speed manual, non-synchromesh transaxle with integral final drive unit. Two-piece casing.

Gear ratios: First - 3.60; second - 2.07; third - 1.25; fourth - 0.80; reverse - 6.60.

Final drive ratio: 4.43:1.

BRAKES

Cable-operated drums on all four wheels.

STEERING

Worm and nut.

SUSPENSION

Front: Fully independent with transverse, multi-leaf torsion bars and telescopic shock absorbers. King- and link-pin design.

Rear: Fully independent swing-axle with twin solid torsion bars and lever arm shock absorbers.

WHEELS AND TYRES

4J x 16in pressed steel wheels. 5.20 x 16 cross-ply tyres.

DIMENSIONS

Length: 4070mm (13ft 4.2in).

Width: 1540mm (5ft 0.6in).

Height: 1500mm (4ft 11in).

Wheelbase: 2400mm (7ft 10.5in).

Dry weight: 780kg (1720lb).

PERFORMANCE

Maximum speed: 97km/h (60mph).

Acceleration: 0–96km/h (60mph): c27sec.

Fuel consumption: n/a.

NUMBER BUILT

(1948) 19,244

1951

Export Saloon

During the 1950s, most vehicles were generally still very plain in their appearance and the Volkswagen saloon, even in its export guise, was no exception. Because of this, there developed a whole industry dedicated to producing all kinds of accessories designed to appeal to owners who wished to personalize their cars. The accessories seen on this 1951 Export model are typical of the era. Many were functional, such as the roof rack to allow more luggage to be carried, and the mudflaps to protect the bodywork. Others, such as the exhaust trim, were intended solely to add a little glamour to what was otherwise still a very modestly equipped family car.

Left The export models featured polished aluminium side trim and plated door handles, hubcaps and other trim. Note the colour-keyed hubcap crests and bumper.

Right Period Bosch spot and fog lamps help to make night driving a little more pleasurable. VWs were never renowned for the efficiency of their headlights.

Left This 1951 model has been fitted with many period accessories, a popular pastime in the days when cars were still very modestly equipped. Note the Bosch reversing light and the genuine VW accessory mudflaps. By the very early 1950s, the Beetle had grown to be more stylish, with chrome-plated bumpers adding a little glamour to the otherwise basic saloon.

Above The spare wheel was carried behind the front valance, ahead of the fuel tank. This vehicle has been fitted with a Hazet spare wheel tool kit which clipped into the wheel centre and contained most tools necessary to carry out roadside repairs. Note the accessory "eyebrows" fitted to the headlamps. These were popular additions and were intended to improve the efficiency of the lights.

Bottom left These vents in the front quarter-panels were unique to Beetles built between January 1951 and October 1952.

Above Note the Becker Monza radio with clock, accessory VDM steering wheel and the bakelite covers to the glove boxes. The Bambus parcel shelf is a practical addition.

Above right The semaphore turn signals have a grooved cover which was colour-keyed to the main bodywork. Semaphores are the same on each side of the vehicle.

Left Marketed by Oettinger in Germany, the Okrasa engine conversion boosted output to 48bhp, allowing the Beetle to reach 120km/h (75mph). The kit included dual carburettors and special cylinder heads.

ENGINE

Oettinger-converted horizontally opposed, air-cooled four cylinder.

Construction: Two-piece cast Elektron-alloy crankcase split vertically with separate cast-iron cylinders and cast aluminium-alloy pistons. Four main bearings. Cast aluminium Okrasa cylinder heads with separate inlet ports.

Bore and stroke: 75mm x 69.5mm.

Capacity: 1295cc (79ci).

Valves: Pushrod operated overhead.

Compression ratio: 6.5:1.

Fuel system: Mechanical fuel pump; dual Solex 32PBI carburettors.

Maximum power: 48bhp (56 US hp) at 4,200rpm.

Maximum torque: 66lb ft at 2,100rpm.

TRANSMISSION

Four-speed manual, non-synchromesh transaxle with integral final drive unit. Two-piece casing.

Gear ratios: First - 3.60; second - 2.07; third - 1.25; fourth - 0.80; reverse - 6.60.

Final drive ratio: 4.43:1.

BRAKES

Hydraulically-operated drums on all four wheels.

STEERING

Worm and nut.

SUSPENSION

Front: Fully independent with transverse, multi-leaf torsion bars and telescopic shock absorbers. King- and link-pin design.

Rear: Fully independent swing-axle with twin solid torsion bars and telescopic shock absorbers.

WHEELS AND TYRES

4J x 16in pressed steel wheels. 5.20 x 16 cross-ply tyres.

DIMENSIONS

Length: 4070mm (13ft 4.2in).

Width: 1540mm (5ft 0.6in).

Height: 1500mm (4ft 11in).

Wheelbase: 2400mm (7ft 10.5in).

Dry weight: 780kg (1720lb).

PERFORMANCE

Maximum speed: 120km/h (75mph).

Acceleration: 0–96km/h (60mph): 18.5sec.

Fuel consumption: 8lts/100km (30mpg).

NUMBER BUILT

(1951) 93,709

Stoll Coupé

Throughout the 1950s, many coachbuilding companies tried their hand at building special bodies to suit the Beetle chassis and running gear. Among the best-known of these are Hebmüller, whose two-seat roadster gained official blessing from the VW factory, and Rometsch, whose stylish coupés proved very popular. There were also many one-off creations and this, the unique Stoll Coupé, was built for a wealthy customer who, in 1952, decided that he wanted a Beetle which would stand out from the crowd. The Stoll conversion consisted of modifying the conventional saloon body into a four-seat coupé with a distinctive "humped-back" profile.

Above The Stoll coupé is unique, but typical of the lengths people would go to in order to make their Volkswagen stand out from the crowd. In the 1950s, many coachbuilders produced special-bodied Beetles in one form or another.

Left Only in profile is it possible to appreciate fully the lines of the Stoll coupé. Its somewhat hump-backed appearance is debatably less pleasing than that of the regular Beetle but it still retains an elegance all of its own. The conversion did little to improve the space available to the rear-seat passengers! Although the factory never offered two-tone paint (except on the cabriolet models), the combination of tan and ivory is particularly attractive in this instance.

Above left   The small, round horn grilles were first used in 1950. The design was superseded in 1953 by an oval-shaped grille. The horn was now located behind the left-hand grille (until 1950 it had been exposed), the other grille being a dummy. Note accessory headlamp cowls.

Above right   The Wolfsburg crest first appeared in 1951. However, the Stoll has been fitted with a rare Australian version of the factory coat of arms. Note the cast-aluminium bonnet handle.

Above The interior of the Stoll is equipped with many period accessories: Petri steering wheel; glove box covers; 100,000km badge; St Christopher medallion, etc. Note the small round heater outlet located close to the floor – the aluminium trim can be clearly seen.

Above   The seats have been retrimmed in leather – this was not a factory
option but specified by the original owner when the coupé was executed.
Note one-piece door glass.

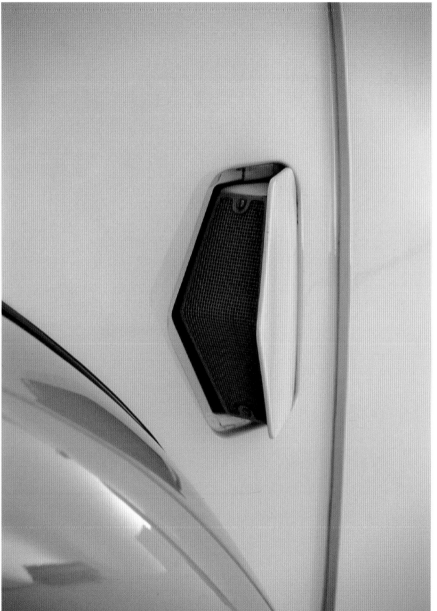

Above left   To improve the ventilation, the leading edge of the door windows were notched – this allowed the window to be wound down slightly for ventilation without causing discomfort to the passengers.

Above right   First seen in 1951, the infamous "crotch-coolers" were intended to provide ventilation but, instead, created an uncomfortable draught inside the car. The feature only lasted just under two years.

Left The engine is the basic 1131cc, 25bhp unit which was the mainstay of the Volkswagen range until 1954. In order to fit the engine under the coupé bodywork, the air-filter has been relocated to the left of the engine – the same modification was necessary on the Hebmüller models. Note the lack of sound-proofing on the bulkhead and the position of the fusebox for the rear lights.

ENGINE

Horizontally opposed, air-cooled four cylinder.

Construction: Two-piece cast magnesium-alloy crankcase split vertically with separate cast-iron cylinders and cast aluminium-alloy pistons. Four main bearings. Cast aluminium cylinder heads with siamesed inlet ports.

Bore and stroke: 75mm x 64mm

Capacity: 1131cc (69ci).

Valves: Pushrod operated overhead.

Compression ratio: 5.8:1.

Fuel system: Mechanical fuel pump; single Solex 26VFI carburettor.

Maximum power: 25bhp (31 US hp) at 3,300rpm.

Maximum torque: 49lb ft at 2,000rpm.

TRANSMISSION

Four-speed manual, non-synchromesh transaxle with integral final drive unit. Two-piece casing.

Gear ratios: First - 3.60; second - 2.07; third - 1.25; fourth - 0.80; reverse - 6.60.

Final drive ratio: 4.43:1.

BRAKES

Cable-operated drums on all four wheels.

STEERING

Worm and nut.

SUSPENSION

Front: Fully independent with transverse, multi-leaf torsion bars and telescopic shock absorbers. King- and link-pin design.

Rear: Fully independent swing-axle with twin solid torsion bars and telescopic shock absorbers.

WHEELS AND TYRES

4J x 16in pressed steel wheels. 5.20 x 16 cross-ply tyres.

DIMENSIONS

Length: 4070mm (13ft 4.2in).

Width: 1540mm (5ft 0.6in).

Height: 1500mm (4ft 11in).

Wheelbase: 2400mm (7ft 10.5in).

Dry weight: 780kg (1720lb).

PERFORMANCE

Maximum speed: 97km/h (60mph).

Acceleration: 0–96km/h (60mph): c27sec.

Fuel consumption: n/a.

NUMBER BUILT

(1952) 1

Type 1 Saloon

For the 1953 model year, Volkswagen finally decided to increase the size of the rear window from its former "split" design to the far larger "oval". This brought about an increase in glass area of some 23 per cent. There were few other major changes although it is worth noting that the dashboard had been substantially redesigned the previous year, the former two-pod symmetrical dashboard layout having been dropped in favour of a new asymmetrical design which placed the speedometer in front of the driver. Bigger changes were afoot at the end of the year when a new 1192cc, 30bhp engine was introduced, the first engine redesign in almost ten long years.

Right With the advent of the oval-window design, the Beetle was starting to take on a less austere appearance. Note the quarter lights (vent wings) fitted to the doors. These allowed much-improved ventilation but opened the way to thieves

Right The bumpers were now of a plain design, lacking the ribbing of the earlier style. The badge bar is an accessory part, as are the two Hella horns. Note the way in which the windscreen wipers park, favouring a right-hand-drive vehicle.

Left The big change this year was the new oval-shaped rear window, the glass area being increased by some 23 per cent. Note the trim moulding around the window rubber. This feature first appeared on the last of the split-window models in 1952.

Above left The bonnet handle was redesigned, now being a chrome-plated casting as opposed to polished aluminium.

Above right In October 1952, the rear light units were redesigned to incorporate stop-light lenses in the top of the housings. This was a considerable improvement over the previous, tiny single brake light fitted on earlier models.

Bottom left This design of dashboard first appeared in 1952 with the last of the split-window models. However, note the steering wheel is still the old style, with spokes that partially obscure the driver's view of the basic instrumentation.

Left Only minor changes were made under the front bonnet: the stay to hold the lid open was shortened slightly and the size of the fuel filler changed from 40mm (1.57in) to 80mm (3.15in) in diameter. Note the almost ubiquitous Hazet spare-wheel tool kit, a popular, and practical, accessory of the time.

Left This was the last year that the 1131cc engine was used in the export models, although it did continue for a while in certain standard examples. By now the engine had been in production for ten years, first having seen service in the wartime Kübelwagen and Schwimmwagen. Although it could never have been accused of being a powerful engine, it was supremely reliable.

ENGINE

Horizontally opposed, air-cooled four cylinder.

Construction: Two-piece cast magnesium-alloy crankcase split vertically with separate cast-iron cylinders and cast aluminium-alloy pistons. Four main bearings. Cast aluminium cylinder heads with siamesed inlet ports.

Bore and stroke: 75mm x 64mm.

Capacity: 1131cc (69ci).

Valves: Pushrod operated overhead.

Compression ratio: 5.8:1.

Fuel system: Mechanical fuel pump; single Solex 26VFI carburettor.

Maximum power: 25bhp (31 US hp) at 3,300rpm.

Maximum torque: 49lb ft at 2,000rpm.

TRANSMISSION

Four-speed manual, non-synchromesh transaxle with integral final drive unit. Two-piece casing.

Gear ratios: First - 3.60; second - 2.07; third - 1.25; fourth - 0.80; reverse - 6.60.

Final drive ratio: 4.43:1.

BRAKES

Cable-operated drums on all four wheels.

STEERING

Worm and nut.

SUSPENSION

Front: Fully independent with transverse, multi-leaf torsion bars and telescopic shock absorbers. King- and link-pin design.

Rear: Fully independent swing-axle with twin solid torsion bars and telescopic shock absorbers.

WHEELS AND TYRES

4J x 15in pressed steel wheels. 5.20 x 15 cross-ply tyres.

DIMENSIONS

Length: 4070mm (13ft 4.2in).

Width: 1540mm (5ft 0.6in).

Height: 1500mm (4ft 11in).

Wheelbase: 2400mm (7ft 10.5in).

Dry weight: 780kg (1720lb).

PERFORMANCE

Maximum speed: 97km/h (60mph).

Acceleration: 0–96km/h (60mph): c27sec.

Fuel consumption: n/a.

NUMBER BUILT

(1953) 151,323

1955

Type 2 Kombi

The Dutchman, Ben Pon, is credited with being the person responsible for persuading the factory to produce a small commercial vehicle based on the mechanical components of the Type 1 saloon. He realized that there was an increasing number of small businessmen who were in desperate need of a delivery vehicle which offered the reliability of a Volkswagen saloon, yet which would be capable of carrying a higher payload. The result was the box-like Type 2, the first new design to come from the factory since the war. With its compact dimensions and heavy-duty suspension, this new VW proved to be far superior to its many contemporary rivals.

Left   Originally conceived by Ben Pon, the Dutch importer of Volkswagens, the Type 2 was a success story from the very beginning. Based largely on Beetle mechanical components (engine and transmission), the Type 2 featured heavy-duty front suspension and an increased ride height due to reduction gears on the rear axles. This stunning Samba model was the top of the range, with extra trim, two-colour paint and roof-mounted windows. The paint scheme of Chestnut Brown and Sealing Wax Red is particularly attractive.

Right Type 2s were equipped with semaphore indicators up until 1960, when flashing indicators were first introduced. Semaphores were located on the door pillars.

Left Early models were nicknamed "barn door" Type 2s because of the large, hinged engine access panel at the back. The small light in the centre is the brake warning lamp. Note the tiny rear lights and the rudimentary bumpers, which would have offered little in the way of protection in the event of a crash.

Bottom left   The dashboard of the early Type 2 was reminiscent of that of the contemporary Beetle – indeed, the two vehicles shared the same instrument panels. Note, however, that the Type 2 has three panels, the centre one frequently being fitted with a radio, while the clock appeared on the opposite side to the speedometer.

Right   Due to the different driving position, the Type 2's gear lever was much longer than the Beetle's and the emergency (hand) brake lever was vertical. Note flat floor to the cab.

Top right The de luxe Samba models were all equipped with this full-length sunroof, a feature which was to prove especially popular in hot climates.

Bottom right There was no shortage of seating in Volkswagen's people carrier. Three rows of seats enabled up to eight or nine people to be carried with ease. The large window area gave the interior a light and airy feeling.

Left The Beetle's trusty 30bhp, 1192cc engine was called into play in the Type 2, meaning that performance was best described as adequate, but never exciting.

ENGINE

Horizontally opposed, air-cooled four cylinder.

Construction: Two-piece cast Elektron-alloy crankcase split vertically with separate cast-iron cylinders and cast aluminium-alloy pistons. Four main bearings. Cast aluminium cylinder heads with siamesed inlet ports.

Bore and stroke: 77mm x 64mm.

Capacity: 1192cc (72ci).

Valves: Pushrod operated overhead.

Compression ratio: 5.8:1

Fuel system: Mechanical fuel pump: single Solex 26VFJ carburettor.

Maximum power: 30bhp (36 US hp) at 3,300rpm.

Maximum torque: 56lb ft at 2,000rpm.

TRANSMISSION

Four-speed manual, non-synchromesh transaxle with integral final drive unit. Two-piece casing.

Gear ratios: First - 3.60; second - 2.07; third - 1 25; fourth - 0.80; reverse - 6.60.

Final drive ratio: 4.43:1.

Reduction gear ratio: 1.4:1.

BRAKES

Hydraulically-operated drums on all four wheels.

STEERING

Worm and nut.

SUSPENSION

Front: Fully independent with transverse, multi-leaf torsion bars and telescopic shock absorbers. King- and link-pin design.

Rear: Fully independent swing-axle with twin solid torsion bars and telescopic shock absorbers. Reduction gears on rear axles.

WHEELS AND TYRES

4J x 16in pressed steel wheels. 5.20 x 16 cross-ply tyres.

DIMENSIONS

Length: 4191mm (13ft 9in).

Width: 1702mm (5ft 7.1in).

Height: 1941mm (6ft 4.4in).

Wheelbase: 2400mm (7ft 10.5in).

Dry weight: 103kg (2432lb).

PERFORMANCE

Maximum speed: 95km/h (59mph).

Acceleration: 0–80km/h (50mph): 30.6sec.

Fuel consumption: 9.44lts/100km (28.7mpg).

NUMBER BUILT

(1950–1967) c1,800,000

1956

Type 15 Cabriolet

Although a cabriolet version of the People's Car had been part of the grand plan from day one, it was not until 1949 that official blessing was given to go ahead with production. The company chosen to carry out the assembly of the cabriolet was Wilhelm Karmann in Osnabrück, a long-established, family-run coachbuilding concern. The result was a beautifully proportioned convertible which bore a close resemblance to the pre-war VW38 prototype in which Hitler rode at the cornerstone-laying ceremony of 1938. Today, early cabriolet Beetles are among the most sought-after of all VWs and, looking at this fine example, it is not too hard to see why.

Right   Undoubtedly the most elegant of all Beetles, the early cabriolets are also the most sought-after. With the hood down, the car takes on an almost toy-like appearance. The use of metallic paints was widespread by the mid-1950s, by which time raw materials were plentiful. Note the wheel trims fitted to this example – originally the cabriolet left the factory with simple chrome "dress-rings" fitted to the rims.

Right The flat shape of the cabrio windscreen was retained, giving it a distinctive appearance.

Left Production cabriolets had the engine-intake louvres stamped into the engine lid, rather than under the rear window, as on saloons. The folding hood of these Karmann-built VWs was of exceptional quality.

With the hood up, the Karmann-built cabriolets were as quiet and draught-free as a saloon. Note the more efficient exhaust system with twin exhaust tailpipes which was first fitted in 1954.

Opposite, top right On cabriolet models, the semaphore turn signals were to be found on the rear quarter-panels just behind the doors, making them difficult for other road users to see.

Opposite, bottom left The dashboard was the same as that of the saloon models. Note the accessory Dehne fuel gauge fitted to the left of the speedometer. A fuel tap was still fitted as standard, located on the floor.

Above The underbonnet area changed little in the 1950s, only the fuel tank being reshaped to improve luggage space. Whitewall tyres were popular, especially in the USA.

Above The rear side windows could be wound down into the quarter-panels. Note how the chrome-framed window pivots down at an angle.

Left The cabriolet relied on precisely the same running gear as the saloon model, which, in this instance, included the 30bhp, 1192cc engine and four-speed, part-syncromesh transmission.

ENGINE

Horizontally opposed, air-cooled four cylinder.

Construction: Two-piece cast Elektron-alloy crankcase split vertically with separate cast-iron cylinders and cast aluminium-alloy pistons. Four main bearings. Cast aluminium cylinder heads with siamesed inlet ports.

Bore and stroke: 77mm x 64mm.

Capacity: 1192cc (72ci).

Valves: Pushrod operated overhead.

Compression ratio: 6.6:1.

Fuel system: Mechanical fuel pump; single Solex 26PCI carburettor.

Maximum power: 30bhp (36 US hp) at 3,700rpm.

Maximum torque: 56lb ft at 2,000rpm.

TRANSMISSION

Four-speed manual transaxle with integral final drive unit. Synchromesh on top three gears only. Two-piece casing.

Gear ratios: First - 3.60; second - 2.07; third - 1.25; fourth - 0.80; reverse - 6.60.

Final drive ratio: 4.43:1.

BRAKES

Hydraulically-operated drums on all four wheels.

STEERING

Worm and nut.

SUSPENSION

Front: Fully independent with transverse, multi-leaf torsion bars and telescopic shock absorbers. King- and link-pin design.

Rear: Fully independent swing-axle with twin solid torsion bars and telescopic shock absorbers.

WHEELS AND TYRES

4J x 15in pressed steel wheels. 5.60 x 15 cross-ply tyres.

DIMENSIONS

Length: 4070mm (13ft 4.2in).

Width: 1540mm (5ft 0.6in).

Height: 1500mm (4ft 11in).

Wheelbase: 2400mm (7ft 10.5in).

Dry weight: 780kg (1720lb).

PERFORMANCE

Maximum speed: 113km/h (70mph).

Acceleration: 0–96km/h (60mph): 28sec.

Fuel consumption: 8.2lts/100km (34.4mpg).

NUMBER BUILT

(1956) 6,550

1957

Export Saloon (US Market)

Throughout the 1950s, the Beetle was progressively improved in an effort to keep up with rival products. One of the major criticisms of the older models had been poor rearward visibility so, in 1953, Volkswagen enlarged the rear window to produce the familiar "oval-window" model which remained in production until August 1957. Outside Europe, the Beetle continued to sell well, even in the USA where people were used to driving far larger cars. However, to meet increasingly strict regulations, in 1956 VW was forced to abandon the old semaphore indicators on cars destined for North America, opting instead to fit new flashing turn signals.

Left The most noteworthy change made for the US market was the elimination of the semaphore turn signals in favour of wing-mounted flashing indicators. These small bullet-like lights are unique to US-spec vehicles of the late 1950s. The lack of semaphores meant a redesigned door pillar for this one market.

Right To meet with new American safety regulations, from 1956 onwards, Beetles destined for the USA were equipped with "towel-rail" bumper guards – secondary tubular bumpers positioned above the originals.

Bottom left The driver's door lock remained the only one which could be locked or unlocked with a key from outside the vehicle.

Top right The interior light of oval-window models was located on the cant rail inside the car, above the door. Note the passenger grab strap – a useful standard fitment.

Above The dashboards of left- and right-hand-drive models were virtual mirror images of each other, with the speedometer and glove box swapping places according to the position of the steering wheel.

Above left The US-specification rear light incorporated the flashing turn signal – the brake light actually flashed. This style of light was not used in other markets until 1960, when flashing indicators became universal.

Above right Vinyl interior trim proved to be far more durable than earlier cloth. Simple chrome trim added a touch of sparkle to the austere door panels.

Left Even for the export markets, the engine specification remained the same. The transmission, however, featured syncromesh on the top three gears, whereas the standard model lacked any syncromesh on any gear.

ENGINE

Horizontally opposed, air-cooled four cylinder.

Construction: Two-piece cast Elektron-alloy crankcase split vertically with separate cast-iron cylinders and cast aluminium-alloy pistons. Four main bearings. Cast aluminium cylinder heads with siamesed inlet ports.

Bore and stroke: 77mm x 64mm.

Capacity: 1192cc (72ci).

Valves: Pushrod operated overhead.

Compression ratio: 6.6:1.

Fuel system: Mechanical fuel pump; single Solex 26PCI carburettor.

Maximum power: 30bhp (36 US hp) at 3,700rpm.

Maximum torque: 56lb ft at 2,000rpm.

TRANSMISSION

Four-speed manual transaxle with integral final drive unit. Synchromesh on top three gears only. Two-piece casing.

Gear ratios: First - 3.60; second - 2.07; third - 1.25; fourth - 0.80; reverse - 6.60.

Final drive ratio: 4.43:1.

BRAKES

Hydraulically-operated drums on all four wheels.

STEERING

Worm and nut.

SUSPENSION

Front: Fully independent with transverse, multi-leaf torsion bars and telescopic shock absorbers. King- and link-pin design.

Rear: Fully independent swing-axle with twin solid torsion bars and telescopic shock absorbers.

WHEELS AND TYRES

4J x 15in pressed steel wheels. 5.60 x 15 cross-ply tyres.

DIMENSIONS

Length: 4070mm (13ft 4.2in).

Width: 1540mm (5ft 0.6in).

Height: 1500mm (4ft 11in).

Wheelbase: 2400mm (7ft 10.5in).

Dry weight: 780kg (1720lb).

PERFORMANCE

Maximum speed: 113km/h (70mph).

Acceleration: 0–96km/h (60mph): 28sec.

Fuel consumption: 8.2lts/100km (34.4mpg).

NUMBER BUILT

(1957) 380,561

1959
Export Saloon

By far the biggest change yet seen in Volkswagen styling occurred when the decision was made, in August 1957, to enlarge the rear window of the Type 1 models. The result was a vehicle which was far more practical to use on the increasingly busy roads of Europe and North America. Introduced at the same time as this redesign was a new dashboard layout which would remain in use, virtually unchanged, until the 1970s. Vehicles of this era were a curious mix of old and new, retaining the old 1192cc engine, first introduced in 1954, along with semaphores and the early-style steering wheel. However, further changes were on the horizon.

Left Great news for Volkswagen owners was the introduction of the larger rear window in August 1957. This single change made a significant difference to the appeal of the Beetle in days when traffic volume was increasing rapidly. Note the redesigned engine lid, too. Mudflaps were popular – and practical – accessories, helping to protect the underside of the vehicle from damage by stones.

Right If you ignore the rear window there appears to be little different about the front of a 1959 Beetle compared with the older oval-window models. However, the windscreen is a little deeper.

Opposite, top left The luggage area of the Beetle had increased only slightly throughout the 1950s and remained woefully small compared with rival products. The fuel tank and spare wheel took up a lot of useful space.

Left The semaphores were phased out at the end of the 1950s, and flashing indicators would soon be standard.

Above The big news for 1958 was the new dashboard, which was radically different from that of the old oval-window models. This design would remain in use, virtually unaltered, until the 1970s when safety laws dictated a fresh look.

Above left   The handbrake and gear levers were still located between the front seats. Note the small white heater knob – winding it clockwise would turn the heater on.

Above right   The interior trim was much the same as it had been: adequate but not exciting is probably the best way to describe it. A map pocket in the driver's door panel was a useful touch – interior storage would always be at a premium.

Left The engine still remained the same: 30bhp from 1192cc. By now, the writing was on the wall for this venerable unit and a new, more powerful engine was just around the corner. Likewise, the transmission remained unchanged.

ENGINE

Horizontally opposed, air-cooled four cylinder.

Construction: Two-piece cast Elektron-alloy crankcase split vertically with separate cast-iron cylinders and cast aluminium alloy pistons. Four main bearings. Cast aluminium cylinder heads with siamesed inlet ports.

Bore and stroke: 77mm x 64mm.

Capacity: 1192cc (72ci).

Valves: Pushrod operated overhead.

Compression ratio: 6.6:1.

Fuel system: Mechanical fuel pump; single Solex 26PCI carburettor.

Maximum power: 30bhp (36 US hp) at 3,700rpm.

Maximum torque: 56lb ft at 2,000rpm.

TRANSMISSION

Four-speed manual transaxle with integral final drive unit. Synchromesh on top three gears only. Two-piece casing.

Gear ratios: First - 3.60; second - 2.07; third - 1.25; fourth - 0.80; reverse - 6.60.

Final drive ratio: 4.43:1.

BRAKES

Hydraulically-operated drums on all four wheels.

STEERING

Worm and nut.

SUSPENSION

Front: Fully independent with transverse, multi-leaf torsion bars and telescopic shock absorbers. King- and link-pin design.

Rear: Fully independent swing-axle with twin solid torsion bars and telescopic shock absorbers.

WHEELS AND TYRES

4J x 15in pressed steel wheels. 5.60 x 15 cross-ply tyres.

DIMENSIONS

Length: 4070mm (13ft 4.2in).

Width: 1540mm (5ft 0.6in).

Height: 1500mm (4ft 11in).

Wheelbase: 2400mm (7ft 10.5in).

Dry weight: 780kg (1720lb).

PERFORMANCE

Maximum speed: 113km/h (70mph).

Acceleration: 0–96km/h (60mph): 28sec.

Fuel consumption: 8.2lts/100km (34.4mpg).

NUMBER BUILT

(1959) 575,407

Right The Karmann Ghia, whether in open cabriolet or closed coupé form, was the most beautiful of all Beetle variations. The result of a three-way marriage between Volkswagen, Karmann, and the Ghia styling studio, it is hard to believe the car is based on the humble Beetle.

1959

Type 1 Karmann Ghia

Despite producing the successful cabriolet Beetle for Volkswagen, Wilhelm Karmann had a long-held ambition to build a car of his own, as had Ferdinand Porsche. In the early 1950s, Karmann began negotiations with Volkswagen with a view to producing a sporting vehicle based on VW components. The talks led nowhere, so Karmann turned to the Ghia styling studio in Turin, Italy, for inspiration. The result was a wonderfully stylish two-seat coupé and convertible which, in 1955 and following much discussion, eventually gained Heinz Nordhoff's approval. Today, early Karmann Ghias are held in high esteem by Volkswagen enthusiasts.

Right The vents in the front panel are to duct air through to the interior – something the Beetle lacked. Today, early Karmann Ghia bumpers are extremely hard to find in good condition.

The hood of the Karmann Ghia cabriolet was extremely well-fitting. Note the finishing strip across the top of the hood and the small rear window.

Left The air-intake louvres for the rear-mounted engine were located near the top of the deck lid. Note the very stylish Karmann Ghia script and the small tail-light units.

Far left The interior trim of the Karmann Ghia was always better than that of the Beetle. Note the large map pocket in the door panel.

Left The Karmann Ghia wore this unique VW badge on the nose, ahead of the front luggage compartment.

Top right Despite the more modern styling, the Ghia lacked luggage space. However, there was extra stowage available behind the front seats as the car was really only a two-seater.

Bottom right The dashboard was far more stylish than the Beetle's, with extra instrumentation and more trim. The steering wheel was unique to the model and looked far more modern than the saloon's. Note the use of the Wolfsburg city crest in the centre of the steering wheel.

Left The engine of the Ghia models was the same as that used in the contemporary saloon, with detail changes to the air-filter to cater for the lower body line. The battery was repositioned to the wider engine bay for greater convenience.

ENGINE

Horizontally opposed, air-cooled four cylinder.

Construction: Two-piece cast Elektron-alloy crankcase split vertically with separate cast-iron cylinders and cast aluminium-alloy pistons. Four main bearings. Cast aluminium cylinder heads with siamesed inlet ports.

Bore and stroke: 77mm x 64mm.

Capacity: 1192cc (72ci).

Valves: Pushrod operated overhead.

Compression ratio: 6.6:1.

Fuel system: Mechanical fuel pump; single Solex 26PCI carburettor.

Maximum power: 30bhp (36 US hp) at 3,700rpm.

Maximum torque: 56lb ft at 2,000rpm.

TRANSMISSION

Four-speed manual transaxle with integral final drive unit. Synchromesh on top three gears only. Two-piece casing.

Gear ratios: First - 3.60; second - 2.07; third - 1.25; fourth - 0.80; reverse - 6.60.

Final drive ratio: 4.43:1.

BRAKES

Hydraulically-operated drums on all four wheels.

STEERING

Worm and nut.

SUSPENSION

Front: Fully independent with transverse, multi-leaf torsion bars and telescopic shock absorbers. King- and link-pin design.

Rear: Fully independent swing-axle with twin solid torsion bars and telescopic shock absorbers.

WHEELS AND TYRES

4J x 15in pressed steel wheels. 5.60 x 15 cross-ply tyres.

DIMENSIONS

Length: 4140mm (13ft 7in).

Width: 1620mm (5ft 3.8in).

Height: 1325mm (4ft 4.2in).

Wheelbase: 2400mm (7ft 10.5in).

Dry weight: 798kg (1760lb).

PERFORMANCE

Maximum speed: 122km/h (76mph).

Acceleration: 0–96km/h (60mph): n/a.

Fuel consumption: 8.2lts/100km (34.4mpg).

NUMBER BUILT

(1955–1974) 363,401

Type 1 Saloon

The 1960s saw many changes in the Beetle's specification and appearance. The 1961 model year had seen the introduction of a new engine, the 1192cc, 34bhp unit which would remain in service in German-built Beetles for another 17 years. With this new engine came a redesigned transmission which, however, still lacked synchromesh on first gear. For 1962, the most noticeable change was the installation of new rear lights with separate turn signal lenses for increased safety. Many consider these early 1960s Beetles to be some of the best ever made, with reliable mechanical components and excellent build quality, while still retaining plenty of character.

Right The range of colours offered by Volkswagen was large and included many attractive shades. Pastel hues, such as this L380 Turquoise, were popular and suited the lines of the Beetle well. Whitewall tyres add the finishing touch, although they were not fitted as standard by the factory. The sun visor over the front windscreen is an accessory part, as are the mudflaps and door protectors.

Right The style of the Beetle had progressively changed over the years and, by the early 1960s, it had taken on a refreshing new look. New rear light assemblies incorporated separate turn signal lenses, and a new engine cover was introduced to allow space for the larger capacity 1192cc, 34bhp engine.

Opposite, top right   The door handles were, by now, equipped with push buttons to open the doors. New door locks were also incorporated in 1961.

Opposite, bottom left   The turn signals were universally mounted on the tops of the front wings in 1961, the semaphore indicators having finally been laid to rest. The design was first seen in the USA in 1958.

Opposite, bottom right   The Hazet tool kit contained most items needed to carry out roadside repairs. Today, such kits are highly prized among collectors of Volkswagen accessories.

Above The dashboard was little changed save for the addition of a fuel gauge. The ignition lock was now located on the steering column.
An accessory flower vase was popular, while a spotlight was practical.

Above right The new tail lights were a considerable improvement, allowing following drivers to see the turn signals more clearly.

Left The new engine, first introduced in the Beetle in August 1960 for the 1961 models, was a great improvement on the older 30bhp unit. It was not only more powerful, but produced more torque. By the end of 1962, a new heating system would also be introduced.

ENGINE

Horizontally opposed, air-cooled four cylinder

Construction: Two-piece cast magnesium-alloy crankcase split vertically with separate cast-iron cylinders and cast aluminium-alloy pistons. Four main bearings. Cast aluminium cylinder heads with siamesed inlet ports.

Bore and stroke: 77mm x 64mm.

Capacity: 1192cc (69ci).

Valves: Pushrod operated overhead.

Compression ratio: 7.0:1.

Fuel system: Mechanical fuel pump; single Solex 28PICT carburettor.

Maximum power: 34bhp (40 US hp) at 3,600rpm.

Maximum torque: 61lb ft at 2,000rpm.

TRANSMISSION

Fully-synchromesh, four-speed manual transaxle with integral final drive unit. One-piece casing.

Gear ratios: First - 3.80; second - 2.06; third - 1.32; fourth - 0.89; reverse - 3.88.

Final drive ratio: 4.375:1.

BRAKES

Hydraulically-operated drums on all four wheels.

STEERING

Worm and roller.

SUSPENSION

Front: Fully independent with transverse, multi-leaf torsion bars and telescopic shock absorbers. King- and link-pin design with hydraulic steering damper.

Rear: Fully independent swing-axle with twin solid torsion bars and telescopic shock absorbers.

WHEELS AND TYRES

4J x 15in pressed steel wheels. 5.60 x 15 cross-ply tyres.

DIMENSIONS

Length: 4070mm (13ft 4.2in).

Width: 1540mm (5ft 0.6in).

Height: 1500mm (4ft 11in).

Wheelbase: 2400mm (7ft 10.5in).

Dry weight: 780kg (1720lb).

PERFORMANCE

Maximum speed: 116km/h (72mph).

Acceleration: 0–96km/h (60mph): c27sec.

Fuel consumption: 8.1lts/100km (34mpg).

NUMBER BUILT

(1962) 876,255

1966
1300 Saloon

If there had been one criticism consistently levelled at the Beetle over the years, it was that it was somewhat underpowered. In the early years, this was not a problem as roads were empty and traffic speed low, but as the years passed and roads became more crowded, it became obvious that something would have to be done. VW's solution was to build a 1285cc Beetle fitted with what was essentially a 1200 engine equipped with the crankshaft from the Type 3 model. The bodyshell was also redesigned, with larger glass area all round, resulting in a less gloomy interior and vastly improved visibility. The Beetle was embarking on a period of evolution.

Left The larger window area of all Beetles built from August 1964 onwards is very evident in this view. The slimmer pillars helped to give a lighter, more airy feel to the interior. This example has been fitted with an accessory trim across the rear louvres and finger-plates under the door handles.

Right The discreet "1300" badge on the rear was the only tell-tale sign that this was one of the new Beetles with a larger engine. American-specification "towel-rail" bumpers were a popular – and practical – addition on many European Beetles as they gave some much-needed extra protection.

Left The door mirror continued to be mounted on the hinge. Only one (on the driver's side) was fitted by the factory – this second mirror is a later addition.

Top left The windscreen wipers now parked to the left of the windscreen. This was not always popular as it left an unswept area of the windscreen in front of the driver. Note how the new, deeper windscreen glass necessitated a redesign of the front scuttle panel.

Top right May 1966 saw the introduction of a new door handle with a distinctive round push-button. The design of the locking mechanism itself remained unchanged from the 1965 model.

Bottom left The dashboard remained unchanged with the exception of a centre-mounted defroster vent. Volkswagens always had a poor reputation when it came to keeping the windscreen clear of mist, and this expedient was thought to be the cure. Note the half-circle horn ring and the accessory parcel shelf.

Bottom right A new locking mechanism prevented the seat backs from tipping forward in the event of an accident – a feature required by increasingly-stringent US safety laws.

Left The new 40bhp 1300cc engine was a major improvement over the old 1200 unit. The engine used the 69mm crankshaft from the 1500cc Type 3 series.

ENGINE

Horizontally opposed, air-cooled four cylinder.

Construction: Two-piece cast magnesium-alloy crankcase split vertically with separate cast-iron cylinders and cast aluminium-alloy pistons. Four main bearings. Cast aluminium cylinder heads with siamesed inlet ports.

Bore and stroke: 77mm x 69mm.

Capacity: 1285cc (78.4ci).

Valves: Pushrod operated overhead.

Compression ratio: 7.3:1.

Fuel system: Mechanical fuel pump; single Solex 28PICT carburettor.

Maximum power: 40bhp (50 US hp) at 4,000rpm.

Maximum torque: 70lb ft at 2,000rpm.

TRANSMISSION

Fully-synchromesh, four-speed manual transaxle with integral final drive unit. One-piece casing.

Gear ratios: First - 3.80; second - 2.06; third - 1.32; fourth - 0.89; reverse - 3.88.

Final drive ratio: 4.375:1.

BRAKES

Hydraulically-operated drums on all four wheels.

STEERING

Worm and roller.

SUSPENSION

Front: Fully independent with transverse, multi-leaf torsion bars and telescopic shock absorbers. Ball-joint design with hydraulic steering damper.

Rear: Fully independent swing-axle with twin solid torsion bars and telescopic shock absorbers.

WHEELS AND TYRES

4J x 15in pressed steel wheels. 5.60 x 15 cross-ply tyres.

DIMENSIONS

Length: 4237mm (13ft 10.8in).

Width: 1540mm (5ft 0.6in).

Height: 1500mm (4ft 11in).

Wheelbase: 2400mm (7ft 10.5in).

Dry weight: 780kg (1720lb).

PERFORMANCE

Maximum speed: 127km/h (79mph).

Acceleration: 0–96km/h (60mph): 23sec.

Fuel consumption: 8.1lts/100km (34mpg).

NUMBER BUILT

(1966) 1,080,165

Right The lines of the cabriolet are best appreciated from the rear three-quarters. To many, the cabriolet models look their best with the hood in the raised position. Note the horizontal layout of the louvres in the engine lid, compared with the vertical style of those on the 1956 cabriolet seen earlier.

Above With the hood folded down, the driver's view to the rear was somewhat restricted. A well-fitting hood bag was supplied as standard with each cabriolet. Note the chrome frame to each of the side windows.

1966

1300 Cabriolet

Of all Beetles built throughout the years, the most sought-after have been the cabriolets. Built by Karmann in Osnabrück, they were based on the regular saloons and, accordingly, shared all the mechanical upgrades. They were the envy of many other manufacturers, for the quality of the Karmann conversion was second to none. Indeed, it has often been said that if a passenger was blindfolded, he would be unable to tell if he was travelling in a basic saloon or a cabriolet, for there was little increase in wind-noise and no appreciable loss of rigidity. It is worth noting that the cabriolet would outlast the saloon on the Volkswagen production lines.

Right From the front, the distinctive shape of the cabriolet windscreen survived even though the glass area had been increased in August 1964.

Top left This design of door handle shows this to be a car built prior to May 1966.

Bottom left The dashboard was identical to that of the saloon. Note the heater vents in the top of the dashboard and down in the passenger footwell. However, heating was still not the Beetle's strong point.

Above The heater controls were located between the front seats on both saloons and cabriolets. One lever turned the heater on, the other opened the vents under the rear seat.

Above left Part of the reason why the Beetle cabriolet was the envy of so many other manufacturers was the effectiveness of the complex hood folding mechanism.

Above right At the front, the hood was secured with these adjustable clamps. The design was so efficient that the cabriolet was as weather-tight as the saloon.

Left As was the usual case, the engine fitted to the cabriolet was identical to that of the equivalent saloon model, in this case a 40bhp 1300 type. Note the current design of air-filter with its pre-heat pipe to supply warm air to the carburettor.

ENGINE

Horizontally opposed, air-cooled four cylinder.

Construction: Two-piece cast magnesium-alloy crankcase split vertically with separate cast-iron cylinders and cast aluminium-alloy pistons. Four main bearings. Cast aluminium cylinder heads with siamesed inlet ports.

Bore and stroke: 77mm x 69mm.

Capacity: 1285cc (78.4ci).

Valves: Pushrod operated overhead.

Compression ratio: 7.3:1.

Fuel system: Mechanical fuel pump; single Solex 28PICT carburettor.

Maximum power: 40bhp (50 US hp) at 4,000rpm.

Maximum torque: 70lb ft at 2,000rpm.

TRANSMISSION

Fully-synchromesh, four-speed manual transaxle with integral final drive unit. One-piece casing.

Gear ratios: First - 3.80; second - 2.06; third - 1.32; fourth - 0.89; reverse - 3.88.

Final drive ratio: 4.375:1.

BRAKES

Hydraulically-operated drums on all four wheels.

STEERING

Worm and roller.

SUSPENSION

Front: Fully independent with transverse, multi-leaf torsion bars and telescopic shock absorbers. Ball-joint design with hydraulic steering damper.

Rear: Fully independent swing-axle with twin solid torsion bars and telescopic shock absorbers.

WHEELS AND TYRES

4J x 15in pressed steel wheels. 5.60 x 15 cross-ply tyres.

DIMENSIONS

Length: 4070mm (13ft 4.2in).

Width: 1540mm (5ft 0.6in).

Height: 1500mm (4ft 11in).

Wheelbase: 2400mm (7ft 10.5in).

Dry weight: 780kg (1720lb).

PERFORMANCE

Maximum speed: 116km/h (72mph).

Acceleration: 0–96km/h (60mph): c27sec.

Fuel consumption: 8.1lts/100km (34mpg).

NUMBER BUILT

(1966) 9,712

1500 Saloon

This model saw some of the most significant developments in the Beetle's specification: a new, more powerful engine, front disc brakes (on European models) and revised styling all made the 1967 model year a milestone in Beetle history. In the USA, Volkswagen also added sealed beam headlamps in redesigned front wings, as well as updating the electrical system to 12 volts – European versions, however, retained the old-style headlamps and the poor 6-volt system. Visually, the biggest change was the new engine lid, designed to accommodate the larger engine. With more efficient brakes and revised rear suspension, the Beetle was continuing to evolve.

Left   The most obvious change made for the 1967 model year was the redesigned engine lid, which was now slightly squared-off at the bottom. The trim along the side of the body was also narrower than that used previously. Flatter hubcaps concealed new four-bolt wheels on the 1500cc models, these being equipped with disc front brakes – a first for the Beetle. However, 1200 and 1300 models retained the old-style five-bolt wheels and drum brakes.

Right From the rear, the new engine lid was clearly visible. Its more bulbous design was to allow the fitment of the new 1500 engine introduced in August 1966, and required the provision of a new rear valance. Note, once again, this example has been fitted with American-specification bumpers. At the front, the trim strip on the bonnet was thinner than before, but that was about all. However, in the USA, Beetles sold in 1967 were fitted with upright, sealed-beam headlamp assemblies, which required new front wings.

Above Although the basic layout of the dashboard
remained the same, the switchgear was replaced with new
"safety" knobs which were soft to the touch. These were
intended to meet the requirements of US safety laws. Little
else changed inside the Beetle – it was as austere as ever
and long overdue for a redesign.

Top left The interior light on all models remained located above the left-hand door pillar. Note the plastic headlining.

Bottom left New door locks and handles were fitted in 1967, the latter proving to be a one-year-only feature. The new locks were designed to prevent the door bursting open in an accident. Again, pressure from the US safety lobby brought about this minor change.

Top right The turn signals remained unchanged, those at the front being mounted on top of the wings.

Bottom right Although the VW logo remained, the Wolfsburg crest had long since disappeared from the bonnet (it was last seen in 1962).

Left The big news for the 1967 model range was the introduction of the 1500cc engine, which had first seen duty in the Type 2 and Type 3 models. In conjunction with improved braking and suspension systems, this engine made the 1500 Beetle one of the best ever.

ENGINE

Horizontally opposed, air-cooled four cylinder.

Construction: Two-piece cast magnesium-alloy crankcase split vertically with separate cast-iron cylinders and cast aluminium-alloy pistons. Four main bearings. Cast aluminium cylinder heads with siamesed inlet ports.

Bore and stroke: 83mm x 64mm.

Capacity: 1493cc (91ci).

Valves: Pushrod operated overhead.

Compression ratio: 7.5:1.

Fuel system: Mechanical fuel pump; single Solex 30PICT-2 carburettor.

Maximum power: 44bhp (53 US hp) at 4,000rpm.

Maximum torque: 78lb ft at 2,600rpm.

TRANSMISSION

Fully-synchromesh, four-speed manual transaxle with integral final drive unit. One-piece casing.

Gear ratios: First - 3.80; second - 2.06; third - 1.26; fourth - 0.89; reverse - 3.88.

Final drive ratio: 4 .125:1.

BRAKES

Hydraulically-operated discs (front) and drums (rear).

STEERING

Worm and roller.

SUSPENSION

Front: Fully independent with transverse, multi-leaf torsion bars and telescopic shock absorbers. Ball-joint design with hydraulic steering damper.

Rear: Fully independent swing-axle with twin solid torsion bars, rear stabilizer bar and telescopic shock absorbers.

WHEELS AND TYRES

4J x 15in pressed steel wheels. 5.60 x 15 cross-ply tyres.

DIMENSIONS

Length: 4070mm (13ft 4.2in).

Width: 1540mm (5ft 0.6in).

Height: 1500mm (4ft 11in).

Wheelbase: 2400mm (7ft 10.5in).

Dry weight: 788kg (1737lb).

PERFORMANCE

Maximum speed: 135km/h (84mph).

Acceleration: 0–96km/h (60mph): 22sec.

Fuel consumption: 7.6lts/100km (32mpg).

NUMBER BUILT

(1967) 925,787

Type 1 Saloon

For many, this marked the turning point in Volkswagen design. Gone were the smooth, rounded lines of old, replaced instead by more angular styling, with a squared-off engine lid and tail lights, larger, more substantial bumpers and upright headlamps across the range. The changes to the bumpers and lighting were made for safety reasons as the Beetle came under pressure, notably in the USA, from the safety lobby. Other "improvements" included relocating the fuel filler to the outside of the car. Some diehard enthusiasts felt that the Beetle had lost its charm, while others believed that the changes were made for the better. It is, as they say, all a matter of taste.

Right   The profile of the Beetle had slowly evolved over the years, the most significant change being the adoption of the new bumpers and upright headlamps. Note also the more bulbous engine lid and the larger rear light clusters.

Right There were several major changes to the Beetle's appearance, not the least of which was the fitment of new "Europa" bumpers. Another new engine lid, shorter and more square than before, replaced that of the 1967 models, while new rear lights also made their first appearance. Many felt the Beetle had lost its charm, while others felt the changes were for the better. Sales, however, continued to hold steady.

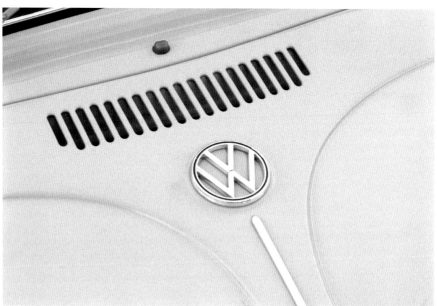

Bottom left To gain more space in the luggage area, and also to meet stricter safety laws, the fuel filler was moved to the outside, accessible via a flap on the right side quarter-panel.

Top right New door handles, with a trigger release, were intended to prevent the doors opening if the car was rolled on its side in an accident.

Bottom right Aware of criticism about a lack of ventilation, the actory finally saw fit to incorporate a fresh-air system.

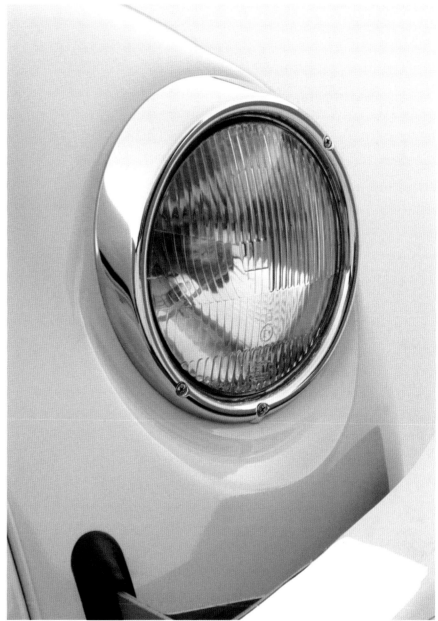

Above left New for 1968 was this redesigned bonnet handle, which incorporated a push-button-operated safety catch.

Above right First seen in the USA in 1967, the new upright headlamp design changed the look of the whole front end of the Beetle.

Left The engines remained the same, although now equipped with 12-volt electrical components on all but the basic 1200 models. VW's philosophy had long been, "if it isn't broken, don't try and fix it". The philosophy had a lot of merit. Note, however, the new valance.

ENGINE

Horizontally opposed, air-cooled four cylinder.

Construction: Two-piece cast magnesium-alloy crankcase split vertically with separate cast-iron cylinders and cast aluminium-alloy pistons. Four main bearings. Cast aluminium cylinder heads with siamesed inlet ports.

Bore and stroke: 77mm x 69mm.

Capacity: 1285cc (78.4ci).

Valves: Pushrod operated overhead.

Compression ratio: 7.3:1.

Fuel system: Mechanical fuel pump: single Solex 30PICT-2 carburettor.

Maximum power: 40bhp (50 US hp) at 4,000rpm.

Maximum torque: 70lb ft at 2,000rpm.

TRANSMISSION

Fully-synchromesh, four-speed manual transaxle with integral final drive unit. One-piece casing.

Gear ratios: First - 3.80; second - 2.06; third - 1.32; fourth - 0.89; reverse - 3.88.

Final drive ratio: 4.375:1.

BRAKES

Hydraulically-operated drums on all four wheels.

STEERING

Worm and roller.

SUSPENSION

Front: Fully independent with transverse, multi-leaf torsion bars and telescopic shock absorbers. Ball-joint design with hydraulic steering damper.

Rear: Fully independent swing-axle with twin solid torsion bars, rear stabilizer bar and telescopic shock absorbers.

WHEELS AND TYRES

4J x 15in pressed steel wheels. 5.60 x 15 cross-ply tyres.

DIMENSIONS

Length: 4028mm (13ft 2.6in).

Width: 1540mm (5ft 0.6in).

Height: 1500mm (4ft 11in).

Wheelbase: 2400mm (7ft 10.5in).

Dry weight: 862kg (1900lb).

PERFORMANCE

Maximum speed: 127km/h (79mph).

Acceleration: 0–96km/h (60mph): 22sec.

Fuel consumption: 8.3lts/100km (34mpg).

NUMBER BUILT

(1968) 1,136,134

Super Beetle

Although there had been significant styling changes made in 1967 and 1968, the introduction of first the 1302 in 1971 and then the 1303 in 1973 meant that the appearance of the Beetle would never be the same again – or would it? With their wide, bulbous noses to accommodate the new MacPherson strut front suspension, which allowed much more luggage to be carried, the new Beetles looked quite different to their forebears. Redesigned rear suspension resulted in a better ride and improved handling characteristics, too. The 1303 model, seen here, came with a large, panoramic windscreen which resulted in more interior space and improved aerodynamics.

Left The 1303 models were unique in that they came with a new, curved, panoramic windscreen. This improved the aerodynamics considerably, but at the expense of some of the Beetle's long-held character. Also evident in this profile view is the bulbous nose and reshaped front wings.

Right At first glance, there appears to be little different about the 1303 models when viewed head-on or from the back, but note the wider, more rounded front end and the larger rear light assemblies. Note also the extra air-intake louvres stamped into the engine lid, rather like those of the cabriolet models.

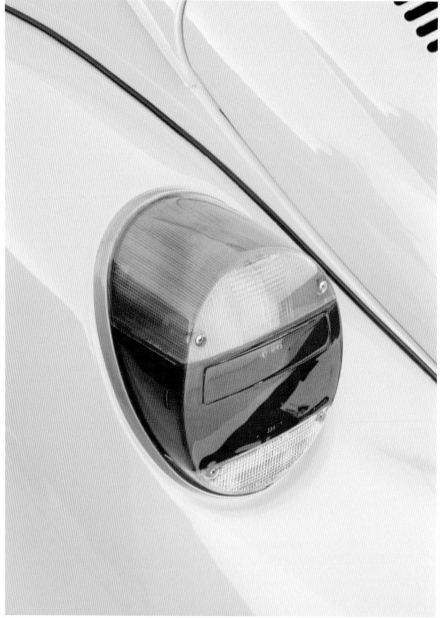

Above left The handbrake lever and heater controls remained conventionally located between the seats, much as they had always been.

Above right Large rear light cluster earned the nickname "elephant's feet", and not without reason. Fitted to comply with American safety requirements, they made the Beetle far more visible in poor weather conditions.

Bottom left   Inside the 1303 models, the single biggest change was the new dashboard, with its extensive padding and relocated instrumentation. A new steering wheel was also fitted – both these major changes were made with safety in mind.

Top right   By using MacPherson strut front suspension, the luggage area could be considerably enlarged. Note the upper suspension mountings at each side.

Bottom right   Sports wheels of this type were a popular fitment on Beetles of this era. They were available with either 4.5J or 5.5J rims.

Left First seen in the 1971 1302S models, the 1600cc engine was one of the finest, although prone to valve and piston problems if not maintained correctly. This engine featured dual-inlet port cylinder heads. Note the alternator.

ENGINE

Horizontally opposed, air-cooled four cylinder.

Construction: Two-piece cast magnesium-alloy crankcase split vertically with separate cast-iron cylinders and cast aluminium-alloy pistons. Four main bearings. Cast aluminium cylinder heads with separate inlet ports.

Bore and stroke: 85.5mm x 69mm.

Capacity: 1584cc (96.6ci).

Valves: Pushrod operated overhead.

Compression ratio: 7.5:1.

Fuel system: Mechanical fuel pump; single Solex 34PICT-3 carburettor.

Maximum power: 50bhp (53 US hp) at 4,000rpm.

Maximum torque: 72lb ft at 2,800rpm.

TRANSMISSION

Fully-synchromesh, four-speed manual transaxle with integral final drive unit. One-piece casing.

Gear ratios: First - 3.78; second - 2.06; third - 1.32; fourth - 0.89; reverse - 3.79.

Final drive ratio: 4.125:1.

BRAKES

Hydraulically-operated drums on all four wheels.

STEERING

Worm and roller.

SUSPENSION

Front: Fully independent with MacPherson strut coil springs and dampers. Steering damper.

Rear: Fully independent four-jointed with twin solid torsion bars, rear stabilizer bar and telescopic shock absorbers.

WHEELS AND TYRES

4.5J x 15in pressed steel wheels. 6.00 x 15 cross-ply tyres.

DIMENSIONS

Length: 4150mm (13ft 7.4in).

Width: 1549mm (5ft 1in).

Height: 1501mm (4ft 11in).

Wheelbase: 2400mm (7ft 10.5in).

Dry weight: 862kg (1900lb).

PERFORMANCE

Maximum speed: 135km/h (84mph).

Acceleration: 0–96km/h (60mph): 18.4sec.

Fuel consumption: 8.3lts/100km (34mpg).

NUMBER BUILT

(1968) 791,053

Type 1 Saloon

The unthinkable happened in 1978 when, on 19 January, the very last Beetle saloon to be built on German soil rolled off the line at Emden. This marked the end of an era which had begun almost 40 years earlier when the original VW38 prototypes gained the approval of the world's motoring press. These last German saloons were often supplied in Metallic Diamond Silver, like this example which has less than 1,000km (600 miles) on the odometer. In many ways, these last-of-the-line Beetles shared more with their earliest forebears than any other: they were basically equipped, mechanically simple and offered reasonable – but not exceptional – value for money.

Right   This, then, marks the end of the road for the Beetle saloon in Germany – it was no longer built at Wolfsburg, coming instead from Emden. The story of the Beetle in Europe was almost at a close.

Top left   This door-mounted mirror was first seen in 1968 and remained in use to the end. Only one mirror was fitted, to the driver's side.

Bottom left   The dashboard retained the black plastic safety padding first introduced on the American market in 1968. The steering wheel was again similar in style to that fitted to the 1303 models and the early water-cooled VWs. The wheel and the padding were weak attempts at updating a rapidly ageing design.

Top right   The rear number-plate light housing was now made of plastic and featured styling ribs in the top surface. Note lack of louvres in the engine lid – these last-of-the-line German-built Beetles were very basic.

Bottom right   The front luggage area was identical to that of previous models. Note the rubber trim fitted to the bumpers.

Above left Cord material was used for seating, giving the interior a slightly more luxurious feel. Heater controls and handbrake were in the usual location. Note the black gear lever and knob.

Above right Blue trim almost looks out of place in a Beetle, but contrasts well with the silver paintwork. The quarter light (vent wing) was an open invitation to car thieves.

Left The 1192cc engine remained unaltered – there was very little point in making any major changes as the end of the line was in sight. Note the substantial air-filter assembly used on late-model Beetles.

ENGINE

Horizontally opposed, air-cooled four cylinder.

Construction: Two-piece cast magnesium-alloy crankcase split vertically with separate cast-iron cylinders and cast aluminium-alloy pistons. Four main bearings. Cast aluminium cylinder heads with siamesed inlet ports.

Bore and stroke: 77mm x 69mm.

Capacity: 1192cc (72ci).

Valves: Pushrod operated overhead.

Compression ratio: 7.0:1.

Fuel system: Mechanical fuel pump; single Solex 30PICT carburettor.

Maximum power: 34bhp (40 US hp) at 3,600rpm.

Maximum torque: 61lb ft at 2,000rpm.

TRANSMISSION

Fully-synchromesh, four-speed manual transaxle with integral final drive unit. One-piece casing.

Gear ratios: First - 3.80; second - 2.06; third - 1.32; fourth - 0.89; reverse - 3.88.

Final drive ratio: 4.375:1.

BRAKES

Hydraulically-operated drums on all four wheels.

STEERING

Worm and roller.

SUSPENSION

Front: Fully independent with transverse, multi-leaf torsion bars and telescopic shock absorbers. Ball-joint design with hydraulic steering damper.

Rear: Fully independent swing-axle with twin solid torsion bars, rear stabilizer bar and telescopic shock absorbers.

WHEELS AND TYRES

4J x 15in pressed steel wheels. 5.60 x 15 cross-ply tyres.

DIMENSIONS

Length: 4028mm (13ft 2.6in).

Width: 1540mm (5ft 0.6in).

Height: 1500mm (4ft 11in).

Wheelbase: 2400mm (7ft 10.5in).

Dry weight: 862kg (1900lb).

PERFORMANCE

Maximum speed: 127km/h (79mph).

Acceleration: 0–96km/h (60mph): 22sec.

Fuel consumption: 8.31lts/100km (34mpg).

NUMBER BUILT

(1978) 271,673

Above Sports wheels were fitted to many of the last cabriolets to leave the production line. Note how the hood could be raised but all the side glass lowered for a pillarless look.

Right In many ways, the last of the cabriolets were some of the most elegant of all Beetles. The curved windscreen somehow seemed to suit the lines of the cabriolet better than it did those of the saloon. The hood frame had been further redesigned to allow the hood to sit lower when folded, thereby giving the driver a better view to the rear. Headrests were another feature dictated by the American safety lobby. Metallic paintwork and a pale-coloured hood gave these late cabriolets a distinctive look which made them appeal to people from every walk of life. They were indeed a classless car and a classic in every sense.

Type 1 Cabriolet

Although the last German saloon may have been built in 1978, the cabriolet continued to be produced at Osnabrück until 10 January 1980 – almost two years to the day after the last saloon left Emden. It is a measure of the cabriolet's importance to Volkswagen that it remained in production for so long after the basic Beetle. The majority of these cars found their way to export markets, notably the USA where there was still a steady market. However, the writing was on the wall for the Beetle as far as Germany was concerned, for all thoughts had now turned towards production of the water-cooled cars: Golf, Scirocco and Polo.

Right From the rear, the most
obvious sign of change was the
single exhaust tailpipe and the
discreet "Fuel Injection" badging.
At the front, note the air-intake grille
under the front bumper – this was
provided to allow air into the optional
air-conditioning system, which was
mounted behind the valance at the
rear of the car.

Above right The interior trim was little different to that of the last of the saloon models, with the exception of the colour choice. Special versions of the cabriolet were available with all-white interiors and matching hoods.

Top left   Once again, the turn signals could be found located on the top of the front wings on this 1979 model.

Bottom left   The dashboard of the cabriolet was virtually identical to that of the 1303 saloon. Note the wood-effect trim across the dashboard and the small rectangular clock located to the right of the steering wheel.

Top right   Late-model cabriolets were equipped with this combined mirror and interior courtesy light.

Bottom right   To meet American safety regulations, the Beetle was equipped with so-called "5mph impact" bumpers, designed to withstand a low-speed knock.

Left In order to meet the stringent anti-emission regulations ("smog laws") in the USA, Volkswagen equipped the Beetle engine with a complex fuel-injection system. The system was not the success Volkswagen had hoped for, resulting in increased fuel consumption. Long-term reliability was also brought into question.

ENGINE

Horizontally opposed, air-cooled four cylinder.

Construction: Two-piece cast magnesium-alloy crankcase split vertically with separate cast-iron cylinders and cast aluminium-alloy pistons. Four main bearings. Cast aluminium cylinder heads with separate inlet ports.

Bore and stroke: 85.5mm x 69mm.

Capacity: 1584cc (96.6ci).

Valves: Pushrod operated overhead.

Compression ratio: 7.5:1.

Fuel system: Bosch AFC fuel-injection system.

Maximum power: 50bhp (53 US hp) at 4,200rpm.

Maximum torque: 72lb ft at 2,800rpm.

TRANSMISSION

Fully-synchromesh, four-speed manual transaxle with integral final drive unit. One-piece casing.

Gear ratios: First - 3.78; second - 2.06; third - 1.32; fourth - 0.89; reverse - 3.79.

Final drive ratio: 4.125:1.

BRAKES

Hydraulically-operated discs (front), drums (rear).

STEERING

Rack and pinion.

SUSPENSION

Front: Fully independent with MacPherson strut coil springs and dampers. Steering damper.

Rear: Fully independent four-jointed with twin solid torsion bars, rear stabilizer bar and telescopic shock absorbers.

WHEELS AND TYRES

4.5J x 15in pressed steel wheels. 6.00 x 15 cross-ply tyres.

DIMENSIONS

Length: 4150mm (13ft 7.4in).

Width: 1549mm (5ft 1in).

Height: 1501mm (4ft 11in).

Wheelbase: 2400mm (7ft 10.5in).

Dry weight: 870kg (1918lb).

PERFORMANCE

Maximum speed: 135km/h (84mph).

Acceleration: 0–96km/h (60mph): 18.4sec.

Fuel consumption: 8.8lts/100km (32mpg).

NUMBER BUILT

(1979) 19,569 – Cabriolets

Below Although it was temporarily joined by the Brazilian Beetle during its later life, it was the Mexican version that finally saw Beetle production come to an end.

1990
Mexican Type 1

The Beetle may have ground to a halt in Germany, but in South America there was still a steadily increasing demand for this no-frills transportation. Production continued apace at the Puebla plant, soon to be followed, once again, by production in Brazil. These South American Beetles may not have had quite the charm and simplicity – or, it can be argued, the build quality – of their German brethren, but they were Beetles through and through. Modern laws forced such things as fuel-injection (Brazil) and safety steering wheels on them but beneath the surface lay the traditional VW values of simplicity, ruggedness, reliability and economy.

Above   There was still little to distinguish the South American Beetles from their European brethren for, at first sight, both appeared to be identical to the typical 1970s Beetle.

Right From front or rear, there is little to distinguish this from any Beetle built in Germany. Mexican Beetles were equipped with 1600cc engines which produced 44bhp at 4,000rpm. The lowly 6.6:1 compression ratio allowed poor-quality locally refined fuel to be used without problem.

Top left   The interior trim was somewhat more luxurious than the average European Beetle, with a brushed velour material being used on the seats. Note the plastic-covered dashboard and the unique steering wheel design.

Bottom left   Sealed-beam headlamps and bumper-mounted turn signals gave the Mexican Beetle the appearance of a late-model European car. Bumpers are chrome-plated Europa-style.

Top right   Rear light assemblies used on the Mexican Beetles were similar to those fitted to European-built models produced from 1973. The "elephant's feet" design was large enough to satisfy the most stringent regulations, even if the lights did little to enhance the vehicle's lines. Surrounds and housing are moulded from plastic to reduce production costs.

Bottom right   Headrests were fitted as standard to comply with safety regulations worldwide. Note the door-mounted rear-view mirror and the rear-seat passenger grab strap.

ENGINE

Horizontally opposed, air-cooled four cylinder.

Construction: Two-piece cast magnesium-alloy crankcase split vertically with separate cast-iron cylinders and cast aluminium-alloy pistons. Four main bearings. Cast aluminium cylinder heads with siamesed inlet ports.

Bore and stroke: 77mm x 69mm.

Capacity: 1584cc (96.6ci).

Valves: Pushrod operated overhead.

Compression ratio: 6.6:1.

Fuel system: Mechanical fuel pump; single Brosol downdraught carburettor.

Maximum power: 44bhp (53 US hp) at 4,000rpm.

Maximum torque: 72lb ft at 2,000rpm.

TRANSMISSION

Fully-synchromesh, four-speed manual transaxle with integral final drive unit. One-piece casing.

Gear ratios: First - 3.80; second - 2.06; third - 1.32; fourth - 0.89; reverse - 3.88.

Final drive ratio: 4.375:1.

BRAKES

Hydraulically-operated drums on all four wheels.

STEERING

Worm and roller.

SUSPENSION

Front: Fully independent with transverse, multi-leaf torsion bars and telescopic shock absorbers. Ball-joint design with hydraulic steering damper.

Rear: Fully independent swing-axle with twin solid torsion bars and telescopic shock absorbers.

WHEELS AND TYRES

4J x 15in pressed steel wheels. 155 x 15 radial-ply tyres.

DIMENSIONS

Length: 4060mm (13ft 3.8in).

Width: 1550mm (5ft 1in).

Height: 1500mm (4ft 11in).

Wheelbase: 2400mm (7ft 10.5in).

Dry weight: 820kg (1808lb).

PERFORMANCE

Maximum speed: 127km/h (79mph).

Acceleration: 0–96km/h (60mph): 22sec.

Fuel consumption: 8.3lts/100km (34mpg).

NUMBER BUILT

1,691,542

the details

Throughout the life of the Beetle, there have been many thousands of changes made in an effort to improve the product. Some have been significant, such as introducing a one-piece rear window in 1953, or a curved windscreen late in 1972, while others have been relatively minor, such as fitting new dashboard knobs for 1967. In this appendix, we show several of the more important modifications made to the Volkswagen, including a look at the many engines which have been fitted over the years. Please note, however, that the year headings below the photographs refer to the particular vehicle shown, not necessarily the year any change was first made.

Engines

One of the principal reasons behind the Beetle's success was the engine: an air-cooled, horizontally-opposed four-cylinder unit mounted at the rear of the car. Designed to be a low-revving unit which, without water, could neither freeze nor boil, the VW engine soon earned itself an enviable reputation for reliability. In wartime, even when subjected to all manner of abuse from heavy-footed military personnel, the little gem of a motor kept on going. More than 75 years after its original pre-war incarnation, an air-cooled flat-four powered the last of the South American-built Beetles, although by that time it boasted such refinements as hydraulic lifters and fuel injection. No other engine in motoring history had been so successful for so long.

1938 Saloon The first 985cc flat-four engine produced a modest 24bhp at just 3,000rpm. Note the single, centrally-mounted carburettor and long inlet manifold. Generator is belt-driven.

1943 Type 82E An increase to 1131cc in early 1943 resulted in a small power increase to 25bhp at 3,300rpm. Cooling fan is driven from generator shaft and is located within the fan housing.

1944 Schwimmwagen The Type 166 Schwimmwagen engine was identical to the regular Beetle engine of the time. Drive to rear-mounted propeller was taken from the end of the crankshaft.

1944 Kübelwagen Type 82 Kübelwagen was also powered by the same 1131cc engine. The air-filter was designed to allow engine to breath in dusty conditions. Note excellent engine access.

1948 Type I Saloon Lever on top right of fan housing allowed owner to set cooling system to summer or winter positions. Note "coffee tin" air-filter – now a highly-prized item among restorers.

1953 Type I Saloon Although capacity remained at 1131cc, a new oil-bath air-filter and revised cooling system helped to make the engine more efficient and reliable. Carburettor is Solex 28PCI.

1956 Type I Cabriolet Engine size was increased to 1192cc in December 1953. This resulted in a power output of 30bhp at 3,700rpm. Increase in capacity was due to larger cylinder bore.

1962 Type I Saloon All-new 1192cc engine was introduced in August 1960, with a power output of 34bhp at 3,600rpm. So-called "non-fresh air" heating system remained essentially as before.

1966 1500 Cabriolet An increase in engine size to 1285cc resulted in a power output of 40bhp at 4,000rpm. As with all engines built from July 1962, a new "fresh-air" heating system was also used.

1967 1500 Saloon The 1493cc ("1500") engine was first used in the Type 2. Recognized as one of the finest engines built by VW, the new unit produced 44bhp at 4,000rpm.

1968 Type I Saloon The 1300 engine continued to be offered alongside the 1200 and 1500 units but, in common with VW policy, was constantly upgraded. Note new air-filter design.

1974 Super Beetle   First seen in 1971, the 1584cc engine featured new cylinder heads with dual inlet ports. Producing 50bhp at 4,000rpm, it was the most powerful yet offered by Volkswagen.

1975 Type 1 Saloon   The 1192cc engine remained in production but had, by now, seen many detail revisions, including the fitment of a more efficient alternator charging system.

1978 Type I Saloon   In Germany, the last of the saloon models produced at Emden differed little mechanically from those built over the previous 10 years. Sadly, the end was in sight.

1979 Type 1 Cabriolet   To meet strict US anti-emissions, Volkswagen fitted a Bosch AFC fuel-injection system on certain models. A catalytic converter in the exhaust cleaned up emissions.

Wheels

One of the most recognizable features of the Beetle has always been the hubcap. The simple, chrome-plated, domed hubcap, which was used throughout the 1950s and for much of the 1960s, became almost as well-known as the profile of the Beetle itself. The wheels, too, have always been very distinctive in design, if rather plain by comparison with those of other makes of car, the large diameter being something of a Beetle trademark.

1938 The VW38 models were fitted with plain black hubcaps which bore no logo of any description.

1943 Military models rarely carried any form of embellishment. The 16-inch wheel is seen in all its glory.

1944 The Type 166 Schwimmwagen was equipped with plain 16-inch wheels and off-road all-terrain tyres.

1944 The Type 82 Kübelwagen could often be seen wearing these "nipple" hubcaps bearing the KdF logo.

1948 The first post-war Beetles came with domed hubcaps which featured a large VW logo stamped in the centre.

1951 With the introduction of the export models in 1949, a chromed hubcap with a small logo became available.

1953   In October 1952 the wheel size was reduced to 15 inches. The design of the hubcap remained unchanged.

1956   Cabriolets came from the factory with chrome trim rings fitted. Shown here is an accessory item.

1957   Whitewall tyres were never offered by the factory as a standard fitment. However, they were popular in the USA.

1962   This was the last year that VWs came with a painted hubcap logo. From now on the hubcaps would be plain.

1966   The flat hubcap used on the Type 3 models was fitted to the Beetle in 1966. Note correct cabriolet trim ring.

1967   With the availability of disc brakes from August 1966, a new, flatter hubcap was fitted. Note slotted wheels.

1968   The Beetle now came with four-bolt wheels, which required the use of the new flat hubcap.

1974   Sports wheels were fitted to several Beetles in the 1970s, varying in width from 4.5J to 5.5J, according to model.

Headlights

At first glance, there only appears to have been one redesign of the Beetle headlight assembly, this taking place in the mid-1960s when the old-style sloping headlamp was superseded by the new "upright" design. However, there have been many detail modifications over the years which can cause confusion among those wishing to restore a Beetle to its original specification. Different markets also often required different light assemblies.

1938 Headlamps used on the VW38 were equipped with symmetrically-fluted lenses. Units used separate bulbs.

1943 The design remained unchanged for the first few years of production. Note body-coloured rims.

1944 A headlamp of the Type 166 Schwimmwagen is shown here equipped with a blackout cover.

1944 The headlamps of the Type 82 Kübelwagen were similar. They were mounted atop each front wing.

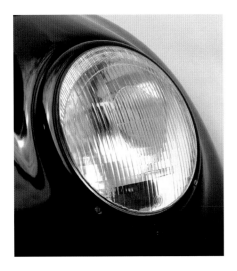

1948 Hella headlamp units had adjusting screws located at the 8 o'clock and 4 o'clock positions on the rim.

1951 Headlamp eyebrows were popular accessories which were designed to focus the light beam more efficiently.

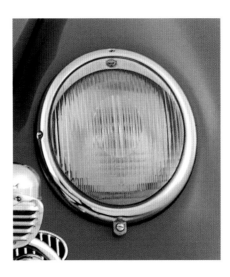

1953 Bosch headlamp units had the adjusting screws located at 12 o'clock and 9 o'clock. Lenses bore Bosch logos.

1957 From April 1955, all US-spec Beetles were fitted with new headlamps which had clear lenses and a separate parking light.

1959 On the European market, Beetles still came with symmetrical lenses to dip the lights straight down.

1966 From August 1960, all Beetles, other than US-spec models, came with new asymmetrical lenses.

1968 First seen on US Beetles in 1967, the upright headlamp was not universally adopted until 1968.

1974 Sealed-beam headlamp units were introduced across the range in September 1973. Note bulbous 1303 front wing.

Rear lights

Until the introduction of the much larger light clusters in 1962, the Beetle was constantly at risk from being rear-ended by vehicles following close behind at night. The small, rather dim, rear lights were never very efficient at the best of times, a shortcoming made worse by an inadequate six-volt electrical system. In 1968, the light units were considerably increased in size, helping to make the Beetle a far safer car. Reversing lights also became available.

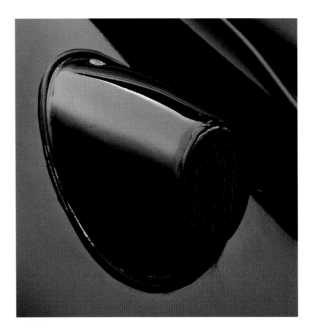

1938   Early rear lights consisted of small glass lenses set in a plain black bezel. Brake light was a separate unit.

1943   The principal difference between this and the previous design was the use of a chrome lens surround.

1944   Military vehicles were fitted with "convoy lights" which enabled following drivers to judge distance at night.

1948   The design of the rear light remained essentially unchanged when civilian production first started.

1951   In 1949 the chrome bezel was replaced by a smaller aluminium one, this itself being deleted in 1950.

1953 In October 1952 the rear lights were redesigned to incorporate a brake light lens in the top of the housing.

1956 In May 1955 a new rear light was introduced on the US market, which incorporated a turn-signal.

1957 The new unit was fitted to all models in August 1955, but semaphore indicators remained on European cars.

1962 The first light unit to include a separate turn signal lens was first seen in May 1961. US models had all-red lens.

1968 To meet stricter safety regulations, a larger rear light assembly was introduced in 1968.

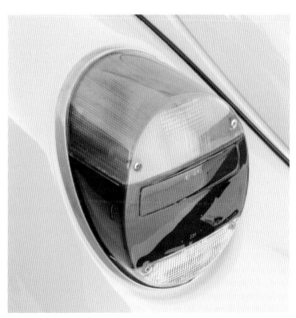

1974 The so-called "elephant's foot" or "football" rear light was first seen on the 1303 model in late 1972.

Rear-view mirrors

Many people believe the design of the Beetle never changed since the days of the KdF-Wagen. How wrong they are, for even seemingly minor components, such as the rear-view mirror, were constantly modified in an effort to improve the overall product. To begin with, the mirrors were very small, reflecting the design of the tiny split rear windows. Later, as the rear window increased in size, so did the mirrors. Cabriolets always featured dual-height mirrors.

1938 The VW38 was equipped with this ellipsoidal mirror, commonly referred to as a "football" mirror.

1938 The cabriolet featured a pivoting mirror which allowed the driver a view over the folded hood.

1943 The "football" mirror continued in use throughout the wartime period in the Type 82E and related models.

1948 The mirror was painted black up until 1949 and was secured to the bodywork with three small screws.

1951 In June 1949 the interior mirror changed to this rectangular shape. Deluxe models were polished.

1953 In October 1952 the mirror grew in size and became more rounded, echoing the new oval rear window.

1956 Cabriolets continued to use a pivoting mirror, although the design was changed in October 1952 to that shown.

1959 The 1958 model, with its new, larger rear window, saw the introduction of another new mirror design.

1962 Although padded sun visors required a modified mounting, the basic design of the mirror was unchanged.

1966 Prior to 1965, the interior mirror incorporated the sun visor mountings. Now they were mounted on the body.

1966 The cabriolet mirror incorporated the interior light in a compact design. Note sun visor clips.

1967 This was the last year that the familiar three-screw mounting was used for the rear-view mirror.

1968 Plastic-coated surround now featured a safety-release mounting, designed to break free in an accident.

1979 The last of the cabriolets came with this somewhat ungainly combined mirror and interior light unit.

Door handles

The design of the Beetle door handle underwent several changes throughout the car's life, many of them due to pressure from increasingly stringent safety laws introduced in the US. While it is true to say that some of the modifications were relatively minor and little more than cosmetic, others helped to prevent the door bursting open in a roll-over accident. For the restorer of an early Beetle, sourcing the correct door handles can be a difficult task.

1938   The black-finished, pull-handle design was first seen on the VW38 prototypes. Note the key-operated lock.

1943   In wartime, the Beetle featured handles which were painted body-colour, in this instance, sand beige.

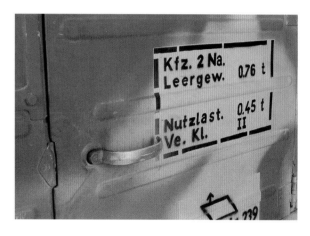

1944   Design of the Kübelwagen was kept deliberately simple, with details like the door handles reflecting this.

1948   The first post-war Beetles were little different from the original prototypes. Note recess in door for fingers.

1951   July 1949 had seen the introduction of the export model with chromium-plated trim, including door handles.

1953   Driver's side was equipped with a key-operated lock. Passenger door was locked from inside the vehicle.

1956 The design of the handle, while superficially the same, changed in August 1955. Note subtle raised ridge.

1959 This was the last year of the old-style pull-handle, the design of which could be traced back over 20 years.

1962 In August 1959, an all-new push-button door lock was introduced, offering greater safety in an accident.

1966 In May 1966, a new door handle was fitted to all models, a design which was used for less than two years.

1967 The 1966/67 handles could still only be locked from the driver's side. These handles are now hard to locate.

1968 To prevent the door opening in a roll-over accident, a trigger-operated lock was introduced this year.

Bonnet handles

The handle securing the front bonnet lid underwent only two basic design changes throughout the 50-year life of the Beetle. To begin with, the bonnet was secured with a handle which had to be turned to release the lock. Then, in 1949, the design was changed on export models to incorporate a more secure internal cable-release mechanism. This remained in use, basically unchanged, until 1968 when a push-button-operated safety catch was introduced.

1938 The pre-war VW38 came with this simple handle which needed to be turned anti-clockwise to release.

1943 The design remained unchanged by the time wartime production had started. Note the lock.

1948 This was the last year that the export models featured the old-style turn handle. Black was the regular finish.

1951 In 1949, a cable-release mechanism offered security against theft. New handle is cast aluminium. Note badge.

1953 New chromium-plated handle was a consequence of an improvement in the supply of raw materials.

1956 Locking mechanism was improved for this year. Cabriolet models featured a lock on the cable-release.

1962 1960 had seen the introduction of a new Wolfsburg badge, although design of bonnet handle was unchanged.

1966 Bonnet badge was deleted in October 1962, much to enthusiasts' sorrow. Handle and lock remained the same.

1968 Due to stricter safety laws, a new bonnet handle incorporated a secondary push-button safety catch.

1974 The design was little changed until the 1970s, when the push-button changed from chrome to black finish.

Number-plate lights

Another seemingly insignificant detail is the light which illuminates the rear number plate on the Beetle. The design of this relatively modest component changed several times over the years, its form reflecting the gradually evolving shape of the Beetle. In the early days of the Volkswagen, the number-plate light incorporated the brake light function, making it difficult for following drivers to see when the VW was slowing down.

1938 The two VW38 Beetles in the VW Museum are fitted with this simple, round combined brake/number-plate light.

1943 The Type 82E was equipped with this unusual beak-like number-plate light housing. Brake light is included.

1944 Type 166 Schwimmwagen came fitted with this combined convoy light and number-plate illumination.

1944 The Kübelwagen had a small light mounted directly onto the engine lid to illuminate the number plate.

1951 Called a "Pope's Nose" because of its profile, this design also incorporated the brake light function.

1953 With the introduction of new rear light assemblies in October 1952, the number-plate light was redesigned.

1957 Between March 1955 and August 1957, another design was used. It was more rounded than previously.

1959 For the 1958 models, another new light was installed, which was mounted slightly higher up the engine lid.

1966 First seen late in 1963, this wider, more angular design gave a whole new look to the back end of a Beetle.

1967 Although superficially the same, the light unit fitted to 1967 models was new, due to the redesigned engine lid.

1968 A redesigned, shorter and more bulbous engine lid required another minor alteration to the light unit.

1974 Despite other changes made to the engine lid of the 1303 model, the number-plate unit remained unchanged.

1979 The last Beetles to be built in Germany, the cabriolet models, all featured this same number-plate light.

Turn signals

From the days of the earliest prototypes, the People's Car had been fitted with turn signals of one form or another, the VW30 having them incorporated into the front quarter-panels, ahead of the doors. When the KdF-Wagen was launched, it appeared with semaphore signals in the door "B" pillars. It was not until 1956 that flashing turn signals first appeared, and then only on the US market. It was in the 1960s that European models were so equipped.

1938 The semaphores on this example were housed in separate boxes mounted on the front quarter-panel.

1943 Type 82E used separate turn signals, despite the earlier KdF-Wagen being seen with pillar-mounted semaphores.

1948 The first pillar-mounted semaphores were made in left- and right-hand configurations.

1951 Later semaphores were not sided. Until the 1952 model, all semaphores came with grooved covers, like this.

1953 A new, smooth semaphore was featured on all oval-window models. The covers were painted body colour.

1956 As there were no true door pillars, cabriolet models had the semaphores located in the rear quarter-panels.

1957 For the US market, all 1956 to 1958 models featured small bullet-shaped turn signals located on front wing.

1962 With the phasing out of semaphores for 1961 models, all Beetles featured these wing-mounted indicators.

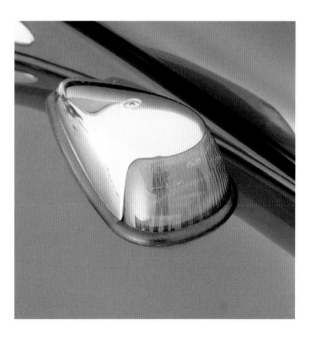

1966 From October 1963 the front turn signal was increased in size to meet new laws. The design lasted for many years.

Dashboards

Nobody could ever accuse the Volkswagen Beetle of being a luxurious car. As soon as you sit behind the wheel, it becomes obvious from the design of the dashboard of most models that this was a vehicle built down to a price. However, this is not to suggest that the Beetle's dashboard lacks style for, regardless of year (with the possible exception of those vehicles built in the mid- to late 1970s), there has always been a certain timeless simplicity which makes it so endearing to its owners. The VW designers certainly knew what they were doing: who else could have made a painted steel dashboard look so appealing? With minimal instrumentation providing all the necessary information, what more could a Volkswagen driver possibly need?

1938　The VW38 set the style for Beetle dashboards for the next 14 years. The simple two-pod design housed the speedometer on the left. A gear-shift pattern appeared to its right.

1943　Little change here except for the KdF logo blanking plate to the right of the speedometer. Note the two open glove boxes on either side of the dashboard and the minimal controls.

1944 The Type 166 Schwimmwagen was a different matter altogether, offering no home comforts. Note the extra levers on the floor to engage the all-terrain gear and/or the propeller.

1944 The Type 82 Kübelwagen was no less austere than its military stablemate. The dashboard housed a speedometer, the electrical switch-gear and a pair of fuse boxes.

1948 Post-war versions of the Beetle looked little different to the last of the pre-war prototypes. Note VW logo in place of original KdF marking and the simple three-spoke wheel.

1953 In October 1952 the dashboard was completely redesigned, with an asymmetrical layout reflecting whether the car was left- or right-hand drive. Note export steering wheel.

1956 The export steering wheel was redesigned in August 1955 to allow the driver to read the speedometer more easily. The fuel gauge is a non-standard accessory made by Dehne.

1959 From August 1957, the Beetle began to evolve at a greater rate than ever before, with a new rear window and a totally redesigned dashboard. Note the absence of a fuel gauge.

1962 A new steering wheel, with chromed horn ring, was first seen in August 1960. The fuel gauge came a year later, on export models. Standard models retained the old fuel tap.

1966 In an effort to help combat the perennial problem of the windscreen misting up, VW added an extra air vent to the centre of the Beetle's dashboard in August 1965.

1967 To improve safety and to help reduce reflections on the windscreen, the control knobs on the dashboard were made of soft black plastic. The ashtray has lost its pull knob.

1968 Three air vents on the top of the dashboard help demisting. A new speedometer now includes the fuel gauge, while the control knobs carry symbols to aid recognition.

1974 The biggest revision ever came with the curved windscreen 1303 models. The new dashboard was of moulded plastic and housed the speedometer in a raised binnacle.

1975 With the exception of the 1303-based cabriolets, the last of the German Beetles continued to use the early-style dashboard layout. Note the new-style steering wheel.

Tables

I Porsche Project Numbers Relating to Volkswagen

Every project which was undertaken by the Porsche design office was allocated a number. Many of these projects never reached fruition, being little more than design exercises.

60	KdF Beetle Project	157	Railway Conversion for Type 82
61	Scaled-Down Beetle	160	Unitary Construction VW
62	Cross-Country VW	162	Cross-Country VW – Unitary Construction
64	Record Attempt VW		
65	Driving School VW	164	6-Wheel Light VW – Twin Engines
66	Right-Hand Drive VW		
67	Invalid Carriage	166	Motorized Infantry VW
68	VW Van	172	Containers
81	Parcel Van Chassis	174	Assault Boat Engine
82	Cross-Country VW	177	5-Speed Gearbox
83	Automatic Gearbox	178	5-Speed Gearbox
84	Twin-Clutch Gearbox	179	Fuel-Injected Engine
85	4-Wheel-Drive VW	182	2-Wheel-Drive Cross-Country VW – Unitary Construction
86	4-Wheel-Drive Cross-Country VW		
87	4-Wheel-Drive based on Type 82	187	4-Wheel-Drive Cross-Country VW – Unitary Construction
88	VW Van	188	4-Wheel-Drive Amphibious VW
89	Automatic Gearbox	225	Experimental Gearbox
92	Type 82 Chassis with KdF Bodywork	227	4-Wheel-Drive Components
		230	VW with Gas Generator
98	Type 128 with KdF Bodywork	231	Acetylene-Powered VW
106	Experimental Gearbox	235	Electrically-Powered VW 237 VW Engine
107	Turbocharger		
115	Supercharged Engine	238	VW-Powered Winch
120	Stationary Engine for Air Force	239	VW with Wood-Gas Generator
121	Stationary Engine for Army	240	Gas-Powered VW 247 VW Aero Engine
122	Stationary Engine for Post Office		
126	Synchromesh Gearbox	252	Gearbox
127	Sleeve Valve Engine	274	Spring-Action Starter
128	Amphibious Vehicle	276	Type 82 with Towing Hook
129	Amphibious Vehicle	278	Synchromesh Gearbox
132	Containers	283	Type 82 with Gas Generator
133	Carburettor	296	Gearbox 307 Carburettor
138	Amphibious Vehicle	309	Diesel Engine
151	Experimental Gearbox	330	VW with Combination Wood – Coal System
152	Experimental Gearbox		
155	Snow Track for Type 82	331	VW with "Native" Fuel system
156	Railway Conversion for Type 166	332	Anthracite-Powered VW

II Type Numbers Used by VW Under British Control (1945–48)

While under the control of the British Army, the numbering system used by the factory was revised, bringing it in line with the reduced number of vehicles which were to be built.

11	Beetle Saloon 13 With Sliding Roof
15	Two-Seater Cabriolet
21	Kübelwagen
25	Fire Tender
27	Open Van
28	Closed Van
51	Beetle with Type 82 Chassis
53	With Sliding Roof
55	Cabriolet with Type 82 Chassis
81	Pick-Up 83 Panel Van
91	Open Trailer
93	Closed Trailer
100	Short-Wheelbase Beetle

III Volkswagen Type Numbers (1949 to Present)

A new Type number had to be allocated to every new model launched. The following is a complete list of numbers relating to all air-cooled Volkswagens produced in Germany.

111	Standard Beetle Saloon (LHD)
112	Standard Beetle Saloon (RHD)
113	Export Beetle Saloon (LHD)
114	Export Beetle Saloon (RHD)
115	Standard Beetle Saloon, sliding roof (LHD)
116	Standard Beetle Saloon, sliding roof (RHD)
117	Export Beetle Saloon, sliding roof (LHD)
118	Export Beetle Saloon, sliding roof (RHD)
141	Hebmüller 2-Seat Cabriolet (LHD)*
141	Karmann Ghia Cabriolet (LHD)*
142	Karmann Ghia Cabriolet (RHD)
143	Karmann Ghia Coupé (LHD)
144	Karmann Ghia Coupé (RHD)
151	Beetle Cabriolet (LHD)
152	Beetle Cabriolet (RHD)
181	Trekker ("Thing")
211	Van – door on right (LHD)
213	Van – door on right (LHD)
214	Van – door on left (RHD)
215	Van – doors on both sides (LHD)
216	Van – doors on both sides (RHD)
221	Microbus – door on right (LHD)
223	Microbus – door on right (LHD)
224	Microbus – door on left (RHD)
225	Microbus – doors on both sides (LHD)
226	Microbus – doors on both sides (RHD)
231	Kombi – door on right (LHD)
233	Kombi – door on left (LHD)